1

London to Fenland

Jasmine Christi

2021

To Nana Y

<u>The first date</u>

The underground was an air conditioned nightmare as fucking usual. I'm not a Londoner, however you can't help feeling like one when it feels oh so familiar being stuck underground on a red light.

The gin in a can had already gone to my head as I hadn't been making time to eat. The best plans are always last minute, so you must not put them off. You buy a baguette for the journey and hop on the next train.

The train journey was just over an hour, which I had done so many times. Each journey consisted of practically the same routine to the exact minute. The first part of the journey you dedicate to telling everyone where you are going (parents, close friends). Once you've said everything you need to say, you move on to activities that waste time. I tend to listen to one album on repeat that I can easily sink into—The Smiths, The Doors, The Libertines. Then I put my face on. I always carry powder with me as I too often find myself waking up somewhere unfamiliar. I don't want men to see me with a red face. There is no embarrassment in putting on your makeup in a full train to King's Cross. If anything, your neighbours will enjoy watching the transformation.

By now, we have about fifteen minutes left, when I check the phone again to tell them that I'll be on the underground soon.

The last few moments as I pull into that platform. This is the best part, choosing a power song. Something sexy, something fast, something that will define my night. You can power walk through the crowds with this song on repeat for the next ten minutes, fresh face of makeup, the gin doing the thing gin does. A quick 30p worth of public toilet piss and to the underground.

Back to the underground, yes. I was stuck somewhere between Euston and Paddington (I know the Circle line better now) with the intention of making my way to Ladbroke Grove before 19:00. We had exchanged several short conversations on and off over the last month. He knew about theatre and wasn't overly eager. He qualified. My initial thought was that he reminded me of Jack Nicholson in *The Passenger*—the beginning part, when he's documenting the desert, or whatever. The colour of the blues and oranges in that film are still on my mind a year later.

I had seen pictures of him on the internet, working as a war correspondent—this is where *The Passenger* came in, I guess. That image of the deep orange sand against a white man. Despite reading the news he was rugged in every way, but completely with style.

I approached The Elgin, he kissed the top of my head and asked me to sit.

His hands were unlike any hands that I'd ever seen. They showed a recklessness and dedication to his way of life, but also a disregard for the basics. His left palm had a three inch scar across it and another smaller scar. His pinkie finger looked as if it had survived a feral dog attack. His hands were absolutely hideous.

I continued on with gin as we sat facing each other on wooden chairs on the street, both at the end of the table. He was a Cambridge boy who claimed to be seven years younger than he was. I had checked his wallet when he went to piss— bad habit, I know. I also slid out a passport photo of him from the wallet. I knew that I would like to peek into his bathroom cabinet. That would tell me everything I needed to know.

We talked about projects. We talked about doing *Huis Clos* as a film together. We knew it worked as a play so it had passed the first test. It was mostly all hypothetical—we had spent an hour in each other's company, sat outside a pub—I was still figuring his story out. So far we had his age, we knew his style and we knew the way that he liked to talk. His voice was particularly smooth. It was the hottest thing he had going. Later in the night, every time he tried to touch me, I would think I'd rather listen to him tell me a story. I had an immense amount of respect for him, doing what he did, and being a free speaker or whatever you want to call it. We need a new word for the 21st century Beatniks.

Later in the night we exchanged stories and opinions on the starving artist. I thought he had money. I certainly didn't have any. It turned out neither of us did. I bought drinks that night.

The first starving artist I had met was the biggest breakthrough for me, in terms of deciding how I wanted to spend my life. I did not plan on starving. A tidy life as an accountant should have suited, but I didn't have the patience for anything other than writing.

Christi does Berlin

The first starving artist. We had met at Cambridge Film Festival. His film was showing and we had decided that the attraction was there. He lived between Berlin and Prague and was doing the rounds with his film *Schmitke*, the documentation of an ageing German engineer who finds himself working on a creaky wind turbine on the German-Czech border. SA had told me they had passed the wind turbine once and it had made the most horrendous creaking noise.

Is that how easy it is? You pass a faulty wind turbine and you make a film about it?

It doesn't work like that for everyone, but God, imagine if it just worked that easily.

This is broken, let's document it.

We seldom document something before it is broken. The change fuels the topic, mostly, I've found. Nobody cared about my underlying issues until they were full-on issues. You get the gist.

Anyway, this romance continued for a couple of weeks. I had just come of age at 18, so it was all very exciting and we had decided to give it a whirl. I found myself on a plane to Berlin which cost the equivalent of one day's wage (I was working as a personal assistant doing admin and whatnot). I hopped on the plane on a Monday, planning to return on the Friday. Please bear in mind this was my first solo trip across Europe. As an 18-year-old, this was the dream. I could tell all of my friends and whoever else that crossed my path.

"Yeah I'm just on my way to Berlin."

The capital of cool, at the time (it's now been replaced by Lisbon, apparently).

So, I found myself in a fifth floor apartment in Neukölln, East Berlin. It was mostly full of Turkish markets selling fruit alongside coffee shops with dirty floors. I darted between the two for most of my stay. How predictable. I don't really know how else to spend time, no matter where in the world I am. The filmmaker lived with another filmmaker. On the front door they had pinned a sign that said 'Directors One and Two' in German. It was worth a chuckle and a photograph.

SA made himself busy with whatever filmmakers do during the day and I made myself busy with a library copy of Fowles in many of the coffee shops a stone's throw from the apartment. No aspect of the relationship was special during this moment, but on paper it looked good so I continued to pursue it.

The moral of the story.

We met his friends at a bar. Here you smoked in the bars, everyone did. This was a lost habit back in England. They had given it up years ago—it was no longer a thing of fashion to smoke, let alone indoors. It had never crossed my mind that I'd be able to smoke indoors ever, so this was a new experience that Berlin brought. The Germans enjoyed watching me hand-roll cigarettes and asked me to do the same for them. Cigarettes were too expensive in England. I think this made the entire process of smoking more addictive—you had to create the product as well as indulge in it. Like cooking your own meals, which we seldom did either.

SA bought us a round of drinks (we are approaching the punch line). We all did a cheers and declared:

"To the state!"

What a curious thing to say, I thought. I followed it up the next day. It turns out they were all on benefits/the dole/state support. The state paid them to exist in their little Berlin flats above the market streets. This concept actually existed. People made films without making money, but they continued to do so anyway. I suppose this was my first encounter with the starving artist outside of films and books. They do exist outside of what you read and watch. They live in East Berlin and they pick up English girls.

So that is it, the first experience of the starving artist, there you are. I still strongly believe you'll write better on a full stomach any day. I didn't know it then, but my own life of borderline poverty was approaching.

My tastes are still influenced by this. You never bought milk or bread because they went out of date within a week. You were too busy making, creating and socialising to commit to something for more than a day. Therefore your diet consisted of black coffee, black tea, rice and frozen vegetables. I still haven't bought milk in years.

<u>Stop trying to fuck me, let's talk</u>

Let's get back to him. We had met in Ladbroke Grove and spent the night chain smoking over drinks. I was on the gin, still. We went back to his. We talked and talked and talked.

Oh, had I mentioned the homeless girl on the sofa?

He (let's call him VF) was one of those rare figures who was all or nothing in every aspect. His home was simple with a couple of posters around. My favourite was a black and white portrait of a couple sharing a cigarette. It was positioned above the toilet.

He tried to fuck me a couple of times during the night. I let him every now and then and he'd slide into me with ease. I carried on talking most of the time. I was too interested in his stories. Anyone can do sex.

He had too many good stories for us to waste time grinding our organs against each other. I will tell him this next time.

Until the next time, I am going to keep our interactions to a minimum. I wrote to him a couple of days after this occasion. I kept it short and attached a cut out of a pornographic image of a woman and a bow from my vintage postcard collection. It should have arrived with him four days after I left. I planned for us to next cross paths twelve days after the first time. Give him time to dwell and to miss me.

I figured that his place in Ladbroke Grove could serve as a good base between here and the Fens. We could even make something meaningful between the two of us in the meantime. I had tried and tested his coffee and his bath—both were good. We were set for the next chapter.

Trains more trains

I usually use commuting time to maintain contact with the important people who are outside all of this nonsense. I keep them outside for a reason. I have too much respect for them.

I called a close friend and my mother to tell them I was well. Trains give you time to do the things you don't really want to do.

Dates are the biggest occasions in my life, now and ever. Sometimes they're even decent, if we go to the theatre and such.

The train journey home often feels like a tunnel to the end. By this time my limbs and mind have had enough. They need to rest for a couple of days. All of my diaries are waiting to be written. It is overwhelming figuring out how I would like to type them, how I want to tell the story and what the highlight is.

The physical pains worsen. I don't eat properly—it's too exciting going on all these dates, I just don't find time. Booze, quick meals, painkillers. I down a large water and a ginger juice on the train. I eat plain, dry bread just to fill my stomach. The excitement won't die down until late this evening when I arrive home to the Fens, and I'll have time to make a real meal undistracted.

As soon as I leave it's like you suddenly don't exist if you don't use the phone. I hate the phone. I don't want to text or call, let alone Instagram story. I don't want to speak to anyone. I want to unwind.

Home isn't so much my home. It has but few purposes—write the diaries, do the laundry and plan the next week.

Some women find a calling. Mine has only ever been dating. It gives me excitement unlike anything else. A lazy excuse would be the attention, but I am not lazy. It's gathering the greater picture of what the world is to you. Their stories up against yours. Intimacy is more than physicality. An honest exchange of words in order to find your other half. I've learnt more from lovers than I ever did at school.

Question yourself a little more.

Upon returning to Fenland I had eight options to consider. I should choose a combination of practicality and attractiveness, then slot whatever else in where I could. I'll stay in London as long as I can, until no more stories come to me and it is time to go home to an overflowing laundry basket.

Right now, I'm in limbo. A life of no commitments and no direction, waiting for something to happen. Personal poverty I suppose induces this. I have no real place to call my own and I end up wherever I imagine I would be the happiest, almost always in someone else's company.

This limbo is very much a hangover in every sense of the word. It is not that there are dry periods or a lack of opportunity, at least not at the age of 21. It is like trying not to be manic, taking a break between all the crazy. A time to unwind on my own so I don't become dependent on anybody else. Also I need clean clothes to avoid a breakdown. Living out of a suitcase is fine for a week, but not much more.

This time is lonely and I often doubt that I will make it back to London when I feel this low, being stuck at my parents' house with nothing to do but laundry. It almost makes me want to get a day job and give up on the life that I wanted.

A friend, RV, told me that anyone who makes anything great is somewhere between manic and you-know-what. But more people end up in hospital than in Hollywood. So, downtime is clarity, for contrast. Don't get hooked on London. You are barely a woman.

I have been dating for many years now and sometimes they throw at me:

"Sure you are pretty now, but what happens when you're 35 and not surrounded by men?"

At least I write. I can gather the stories now, write later. Maybe I'll approach 36 and all will have faded. Then I can reflect, and write about every single man that I ever sat across from. Maybe I'll even start to write fiction.

Learning to write

I have always made excuses not to write. I don't have a desk. My apartment is too small. You think an ideal will form, that somehow something will happen overnight which means you are able to write. Life's not like that. You just have to do it. I do it best when I'm on trains. When walking alone I practise telling stories—which parts I will tell to friends and which parts I should leave out for my parents.

A few months ago I bought a handheld recorder so I could tape conversations. Half of the time I forgot to turn it off, so it recorded entire drunken dinner parties.

I've only ever been to one dinner party, sorry for lying.

Hearing how you talk and how people respond. Writing it onto paper is even more clarifying. So much wasted time. Talk talk talk. I didn't know anybody at the dinner party (I had met a bloke in a pub who'd invited me) but I managed to talk and talk and talk. We all did.

I lost six years of diary content because I felt I couldn't write, or didn't have the correct desk. I can only scorn myself now. I could have typed it on my phone in bed and it would have been perfect. Laziness is my biggest flaw. I don't use time well. I spend too much time in bed or watching TV.

Still I mustn't hold a grudge. 15-year-old Jasmine living in her family home couldn't have written much good. It was just school and my first boyfriend. Although at that age it was a time of everything being new. My first date. My first screw. My first time lying to my parents to sneak out and get drunk in a field. It seems more exciting than anything I could do now. I don't have to lie anymore and nobody really cares where I am, let alone who with.

When I was a teenager and trying to learn to write I would choose the latest frilly word I had learnt and try to write a poem around it. Atavistic, esoteric, etc. Just some new word that I wanted an excuse to use.

By now you can tell I don't write frilly.

No matter which dumb word I chose, these poems turned out so drab and almost always alike—something grey and about the weather.

It is true the English are obsessed with the weather.

Then, when I started living alone with the older lady in Ely, I went for long walks at night. It was down to extreme loneliness. I'd sometimes go to the pub and try to write. I remember one time I took the leaflet from a box of Paracetamol and crossed out words to make my own little story. I suppose that was when I realised you can write anything and it is still valid.

That night I went back with two American Air Force guys to their hotel. I was lonely and I am, still.

You naturally talk about the highs but people are more interested in the lows. Reminds me of something I read by Martha Gellhorn:

"People will talk about the weather rather than hear our glowing reports on Copenhagen, the Grand Canyon, Katmandu. What holds people are disaster narratives, if only because listeners can hardly wait for us to finish before they launch into stories of their own suffering in foreign lands."

I don't particularly want to talk about living with the lady in Ely who kept the thermostat on 14 degrees at the height of winter.

We naturally document the lows. I am trying things the other way around—documenting the highs. Was this all it took to make me a writer? Acknowledging the highs rather than the lows? Either way, it's all fine, I am here for us now. I have no desire to pinpoint one reason that fuelled this—there are many possibilities—but they have no real use.

I have no advice to give other than to fill your time with lovers whilst you're waiting to write.

I tried travelling and moving around. If anything they delayed it. Consistency helps everything, in moderation, ha. Try it over and over. I got there.

I am envious in some way of the writers who can write any fiction that they desire. I have tried to conjure a story, but they are all based on people who have crossed my path, or stories I have heard before. I cannot pluck ideas out of thin air.

When you have to write about yourself, you give parts of yourself up, you expose your life in many ways other people do not. Is it because I want to share? Sometimes. More often than not I just write everything down and I can cut and edit out the irrelevant details.

I keep the uncomfortable, the dirty and the sinful aspects sometimes. I don't mind these—I have committed them and someone in the world was a witness. Anyone could know if their means were right, so I'll just write them down myself, no frills, just events as they unfold.

Canadian boy

I was dating and living with a Canadian writer over the summer, before he left the Fens and disappeared into a cloud of London never to be seen again.

He had a single tattoo that read:

'A REBOURS'

A dedication to his love for Huysmans. I ordered a Penguin Classics edition and gave it a go in the heatwave of 2018. I didn't get it as a whole, but don't think I could blame the heat.

Against the grain, against nature, sure.

I'm a poor young English woman. I can't relate to some pumped up rich Parisian hiding in his mansion. How do people read this? I suppose it could offer some escapism, but I just can't picture it.

I finished without understanding much of what was going on.

The world is too ugly for Decadence to be taken seriously.

I practise decadence from time to time, sure, very rarely but I do shop at Waitrose.

OK. I retract that statement. An ugly world is a reason for Decadence. You got me.

I hate ugliness. In retrospect this is why I wasn't a good enough nurse. I hate going to the bathroom, cutting my nails, cleaning dirty dishes. Actions you wouldn't perform in the company of your lover, I barely want to do alone. This is why I had made the decision to never live with a lover. Sure, you soon fall into habits and become lazy, but that is when it starts to die. I once lived with a lover for six weeks. I soon found myself leaving the toilet door open, not cleaning the bath after I had let the water run out, and leaving dirty cups around the house. Soon after this we ran out of love.

I lived with a greater love (a South African boy) but it worked out better because we kept to ourselves whilst living together. We would lay on opposite couches, reading and drinking. We would quietly excuse ourselves to use the bathroom or to retire to our separate single beds in the same room. We were able to live separate but fulfilling lives in the company of one another. Again, this lasted just short of eight weeks and I never saw him again. I don't care to spend all of my time writing about this romance, but it was my closest experience to bliss, so it is relevant and I have to give it credit. I have to acknowledge the impact it had on the greater picture of my life.

Back to Canadian boy (DM). He took me to the theatre (my first time). We saw Pinter at The Pinter.

I'm still pissed off that he left me for London. Nothing in myself is strong enough to force a man to stay. Nothing.

I wrote to him a couple of times at his new address in Isleworth, London. Isleworth itself isn't very nice but it is close to Richmond and I like the walks along the river.

I still want to pursue him. Turns out VF lives a mere mile from DM's new place of work in White City and six miles from his front door. It's one bus ride. I could walk there in 22 minutes. I know what time he starts and finishes work. It could be easily arranged.

I hope he might stop to speak but I can't be sure. I am just not sure why he left. I would like to understand why. I think he saw me more as a sister and couldn't understand why I was too depressed to be productive.

I have often been called 'the saddest girl in the world'.

If I find myself free at 17:00 I will walk down to White City to catch him leaving work. Even if he doesn't speak there will be no time wasted. I can walk back to VF's house or find someone else to go out with for the night.

Next time I'm in London I'll go. For now, the Fens.

Local lovers

Today I am still in the process of recovering. I am playing it quiet. The phone is off. I am indulging in one of those games again. The phone is in the drawer. No one will hear from me for a couple of days. I don't even feel remotely tempted to check it. I have no desire to contact or be contacted. Everything is fine.

My plans for the week ahead seem to be in place, I just have a couple of chores to do and two minor lovers to visit.

It is difficult to pinpoint a reason why people aren't revolutionary lovers. It is all of the small circumstances added up that lead to either a huge attraction or not.

This week we have two lovers to see:
1. S?
2. MG

S? was the closest of them all to my age. He was seven years older than me, Polish (I love Poles), and working as a video game coder (or something) in Cambridge. He needed attention often and wasn't afraid of letting you know. He blew up my phone constantly with pointless messages that didn't warrant a response of any sort. More often than not I ignored him and carried on with my own day. We had a couple of interactions that did make me interested in him. His story was classic yet still touching. He had a troubled childhood with an aggressive father, Poland had nothing to offer, he moved to the UK for work and was still a little lost after several years of working here and not finding love. He had many great features. He was incredibly generous with his time and small gestures—we always ate breakfast together and he would let me choose the wine for the night. We were brutally honest with each other about how it was going at the time and whatever else was happening outside of the now. He dated often but never anything serious—he was going through a period of being bailed on often. We had slept together maybe twice. He wasn't my typical male fantasy, though slim and classically handsome in the face. I joked that he was my young Marek Grechuta—my favourite Polish singer.

I preferred his voice when he spoke in his mother tongue. He always tried very hard to fuck me. He always wanted to give it a go. I gave him intimacy but in the form of sleeping with my legs tucked between his, the occasional peck on the cheek and making last minute plans together. We would wander around Cambridge with no real direction. Not a serious or meaningful interaction, but one of comfort nonetheless.

MG was underway during this time too. I always had a very clouded image of his personality and traits—he was hard to read and I haven't figured out if it was pure shyness or if he was really trying hard to hide something. He was 19 years older than me, from Glasgow and had relocated here for work—an analyst or engineer of some sort. He had a very comfortable apartment with good lighting in the centre of town. He also had a car. I sold mine. I don't want to worry about a piece of metal when I have a hangover. I'd rather worry about a train.

He was kind-hearted and relatively simple to please. I kept my distance and kept it to a once a week meeting. He was incredibly handsome, a real alpha male. Such a beautiful face and soft Scottish accent. He was great fun to fuck. It made me feel powerful. He really got lucky with life.

We had been doing all of this very comfortably for a couple of weeks and I had decided that the time to end it was approaching. Waiting any longer would cloud things and it would no longer be enjoyable, spontaneous or fun.

I made the date, Tuesday. As I've said, let us preserve this lovely memory and move on.

Rice with butter

Today is a continuation of my quiet period. This time is dedicated to documenting life in my diaries, low life pleasures, long showers and overeating.

I have been managing to sleep in for long periods of time which is a huge pleasure. Uninterrupted, deserved sleep. God, thank you.

A pair of clean silk pyjamas for my rest days and a second pair ready for the week away ahead.

Some days I can sleep in until 15:00, on and off with cups of tea every few hours, but this is still a huge, restful indulgence. There is not much to report on days like this. These days I have to focus on my physical needs and preparations.

However, I did make the time to visit Cambridge Festival of Ideas. A boy from Essex took me out. We listened to a talk at one of the colleges but I daydreamed mostly. We sat by the River Cam and smoked. I didn't fancy him enough, so I took the train home alone before late. Nothing more interesting to report.

I never really talk about money in my diaries. I somehow seemed to have a steady couple hundred pounds, seldom more or less. Whenever I felt bored shitless I'd work every day in a pub or cafe for a month, then quit so I had a few grand to work with.

My spending is very predictable. £100 a week or so on train travel, £30 on food, £10 on tobacco and occasional other expenses like a birthday gift, flowers or cosmetics.

I never outright asked anyone for money, except for when they offered. I was often blunt and upfront about my financial situation—it wasn't stable but I never really worried. I would always accept a sum from a lover to pay for food, trips, the odd contribution towards my train fare. I am happy to accept from someone who is happy to give. I never found myself hungry-hungry, but was bored of rice with butter for dinner five days in a row.

I had decided the nine-to-five could never work around the writing and the lovers, so it wasn't worth a go. My time is too precious to give up for a wage. Life was fine as it was now, anyway. No need to worry.

Glaswegian

Today was the final day of rest before it started again. I had made big plans. It was break up day. No special arrangements have to be made, just the usual routine.

I spent the day lounging around and waited for him to text me. I don't purposely leave it longer than necessary, but I tend not to worry until an hour before. He wanted to make plans for the evening. I had my own ideas but pretended to be an open book.

I was feeling under the weather by the time the sun came down. I had overeaten and overslept.

I was considering what to drink on the train. I decided on vodka. I felt utterly nauseous and sick and delicate so I didn't take a drink. I wore my tighter grey dress with black tights and my yellow trainers. MG had told me he liked these trainers before, on our third meeting he had said.

He met me from the train. He came from a direction I wasn't expecting, so it took me a moment to acknowledge him. He was wearing a smart black coat. I hadn't seen it before. I had only seen him in a casual jacket and blazer. I don't know what he thought the occasion was.

Anyway, I told him I wanted to have a quiet night as I was feeling delicate. On the walk I was still trying to decide if I was well enough to drink or if it was too slippery a slope. My stomach cramps had stopped for an hour so I decided it was safe.

We smoked two joints I had rolled and we drank a bottle of red between us. I had bought it on a previous date and we never got around to drinking it. The red was good. It made me feel better than I'd felt all day.

I laughed at the thought of being cautious earlier.

We smoked on the balcony and he had a habit of massaging my feet when we sat opposite each other. He insisted it wasn't a fetish but it felt like it was. Each time he would reach for my feet and gently stroke them between his hands. He was a great comfort. He had great hands. So many little attractive features like that just added up to make him a solid man. The accent helped too.

We had touched on music but never properly delved, except for the time he drove us to the beach and insisted on being in charge of the music. We started off with The Smiths and then made the natural progression to Elvis. The music was always good.

We ate and smoked, shared an ecstasy pill and listened to music most of the night before he led me to bed. He took the lead and started to rub me down with baby oil, which I thought was a nice touch for our goodbye sex. He had never done that before. We had a really fun time and I slept deeply after.

A vegetarian breakfast with a side of bacon

We gave it a good go in the morning too, shortly after 08:00. I showered. He used Pears soap which I found sweet and innocent. That familiar clear orange bar always gave me a laugh. Who under 60 used Pears?

One of the highlights of staying with him was watching his naked body emerge from the shower—a visual feast. I'm quite fussy with men and their appearance, it's a rarity to find someone really attractive.

This was the reason it had to end. The only focus I could think of was his physical presence. I am growing bored writing of it. Sorry dear MG, I love you as a friend but now is not the time.

I drank a can of Coca Cola for breakfast as we watched pornography on the couch. I charged my phone and double checked my plans for the next hour. MG left for work and we walked down Hills Road together before heading in opposite directions. He gave me a short passionate cluster of wet kisses on the mouth, three or four soft wet pecks.

I blocked his number straight after and walked to the train station.

Then something unplanned occurred. Guess who crossed my path? There she was in all of her glory and beauty. Nana Y!

She was as surprised to see me as I her, at 09:00 outside the train station. I had to create a fast back up story. I try to keep my immediate family and friends out of the nonsense stories that I endure for the writing. The easiest alternative often is that 'I have a new love interest' because it can be dismissed quickly and is never thoroughly investigated until a later date. If you are seen in a new location, the story is simply that 'I broke it off with the last guy because he was boring and now I've been out a couple of times with this new guy'. Easy.

Nana Y laughed and asked if he was handsome. I told her yes. We embraced warmly. I love Nana Y more than anyone. We just get each other. She carried on her journey and I lit a cigarette whilst I waited for my girlfriend HK to arrive by train into Cambridge.

HK is one of these special friends where our interactions can be limited for a year but then we slide back into place each time we meet again. We exchanged stories and pictures of recent lovers over breakfast in central Cambridge. I ate pancakes with bacon and a strawberry lemonade. She ate a vegetarian breakfast with a side of bacon. We perched on the wall of King's Parade for ice cream afterwards.

Spending time with devout friends with history, a history of the friendship, is very important. These people can judge your character more accurately than dates can. They can advise you, and comment on your mental and physical state better than your parents or lovers. These interactions are to be cherished. This breakfast was definitely needed.

Whilst we sat eating ice cream I found myself feeling quite excitable and attached to my phone. I would slyly check it twice an hour as I couldn't resist sending picture updates of myself and HK over to VF (whom I hadn't seen in nearly two weeks). They showed my real side outside of dating and writing—the times when I relaxed and did normal activities with other wholesome young women. I wasn't a drunk, drugged up girl running around from place to place.

My phone battery quickly drained as I hadn't had a chance to charge it fully whilst at MG's. He had even reminded me to charge it, that was how sweet natured he was. I had to make my way home to start my short detox before returning to London.

Back to Ely

I walked across town with my bag from the night before. A small makeup bag with a toothbrush, powder and cleanser, a spare pair of tights, a charger and a book for the train. I can rewear outfits as I am extremely clean and shower multiple times a day. I hate carrying a big bag and backpacks are ugly.

The bag is a yellow tote I wear on my right shoulder. It does start to strain after a couple of hours, after which I have to massage my shoulder to loosen the tension. For a while now I have been considering what it is that I would like to carry on me. I am reluctant to carry ID and credit cards as they bear my real name and I wouldn't want a date to find out that or my address. This could be a serious issue if they wanted to track me down—it would be quite easy. I prefer to give my pen name, Jasmine Christi. But if I ever found myself in a spot of trouble, there would be no ID to confirm my identity. It is something to think about. Too much trouble, probably. Men don't go through women's purses, do they?

I was making my way across the town centre. There is one street where I happen to know four shop owners, so conversation is inevitable. I must admit, it does bring a smile knowing that I will come across familiar faces on my walk home. It gives me a good chance to adjust to my surroundings and home town.

People are always interested in the stories you have to bring and the new joys of the world you have recently explored.

Anyway, this day was a particularly quiet one. I made my way through the town with the intention of walking to my door with little interruption.

However one of the treasured ones crossed my path—a boy I was friends with, a little bit of a nomad. He knew everyone in town who was unemployed. He had a kind soul and always had a story to share. We clocked each other at the same time and went in for a sideways hug. I felt like it had been a while since we had last updated each other, so it was worth proposing a plan.

"Coffee or spliff?"

"Both?"

I got the coffee in and we made our way to the park. I had some leftover weed in my purse and some rolling tobacco.

Now, this boy. He had slept in my bed and been in my home for a couple of days last year. We had a very comfortable interaction with no sexual or emotional pressure. We turned up when we wanted and chatted for as long as we wanted, before parting. I didn't have his phone number, we just met when we met and that was the dynamic. It was a rare luxury in the twenty first century to have a relationship like this.

We conversed about the usual bullshit—finding a job, letting love go, new propositions, the trouble we had found and avoided. Once my stories had run out it was time to leave and begin the reflection at home.

My mind was still buzzing and racing and I wasn't sure when I would be sober enough to safely interact with family unnoticed. This was always the worst part. The in-between phase. Not sober enough to function but not fucked enough to ignore your responsibilities. It is very hard to describe the buzz you get whilst on a manic high. It's the first acknowledgement of the gin kicking in, the reciprocation of good news from an old friend, the reply to an important email—that sort of buzz. It is constant and you need to know how to manage it and not get carried away in the moment.

My first rule is you must put important aspects to the side (things you could easily jeopardise) during this time.

First and foremost, the phone goes away. Compulsive actions will never take you far. Everyone knows they are done without thought and should be ignored and not taken seriously. On my way home the buzz is there. The phone is off for now.

Dinner with the parents

This is the first day of proper recovery. No men. Food, sleep and laundry will be in need of some dedicated time.

I begin with sleep so I don't have an excuse for not completing the following tasks. I sleep in until I can no longer stand it. I find hot tea with sugar is one of the most comforting things during the recovery period. The phone is still off and to the side, until I run out of things to do. I am keeping busy with laundry and writing.

You may be eager to begin something, but whatever the case, you need to dedicate very specific time to it. I usually operate in the middle of the day. I work well in the mornings too, but I find myself with a burning need to leave the house before 10:30. I seldom work at home as there are too many distractions. I mostly work from a coffee shop—free refills and a nice social buzz around me I can dip in and out of. I don't generally tell people what it is I'm working on. I find it very difficult to sum up. I tend to just close the conversation with *the diaries*.

I contemplated drinking and smoking today, but I decided my body deserved to rest and I should respect that. I had two cups of coffee and cracked on with writing for six hours. The phone was still to one side for now. I'd dedicate time tomorrow to making plans for the following week. I had a rough outline of the days and their timings that I could plan around. I was feeling excited about meeting VF for the second time. I didn't know how long I would stay for. I dropped a couple of gentle hints to see what he wanted.

When laptop writing became a chore I decided to switch to pen and paper. I had to write an update to Canadian boy. I had been contemplating visiting his work and I thought maybe I should alert him. I wrote him a short letter outlining my plans for the following week, noting I would be in the area. I sealed and mailed it so he would know to expect me and would have time to make an informed decision as to whether to see me.

I met my mother and stepfather in town for dinner at their restaurant. I ate warm bread, steak with chimichurri and one scoop of vanilla ice cream, washed down with two small glasses of Montepulciano and a Cointreau with ice. I walked home tipsy in the dark and smoked a few cigarettes.

London begins

For the first time since starting these diaries I am questioning the motive behind them. During the highs the motive feels particularly put on—a show, a dance or a mindset that is hard to embody at any given period. The high is similar to the confidence boost you get from that first glass of wine. The warm embrace and the social fuel. The conversations that have no start and no end.

For a week now I had planned to relocate and start my documentation in London. I had planned to use VF in Ladbroke Grove as base camp—somewhere to return to after each venture. I did want to spend time with him too.

After our first venture out in London—and sleepover—I had decided I had to play it cool for both of our benefits. He always dropped me a text throughout the day, usually a witty one liner that I struggled to write an answer to. For example, I texted him a picture of a slice of cake.

"Chocolate tart with bayleaf from my garden."

He replied:

"Vodka with coke from my fridge."

Cunt.

Shit he was good with words in that way. I did tend to reread anything and double-think when I wrote to him, which was a rarity during this period. I even wrote to him once with pen and paper during my absence from London. The longer I stayed away, the longer I realised that I longed for our conversation as a twosome, as a couple—us alone in our bubble.

I figured our first date outside The Elgin was probably my best date ever, conversation wise. I couldn't think of anyone whose words got me off more. But the dynamic at the beginning was too wrong for me to take seriously. I am reconsidering that now.

I arrived last night. It was dark and winter was in full swing. The clocks had gone back the day before. You could really feel the cold. I was enjoying the weather after what had felt like an endless summer heatwave fuck fest with Canadian boy. It was too hot. We would lie around in shorts and vests all day, reluctant to do anything. In winter you had no excuses to be lazy.

I had dropped my bags in the corner of the lounge where I envisioned leaving them for the coming week. He poured drinks—red followed by vodka.

We listened to music. He let me choose the entire time. He never objected to what I put on. Anyway, VF and I had been listening to Talking Heads, Elvis, Nico (he didn't enjoy her whining German accent as much as I do), and it went on for a couple of hours.

I had changed out of my cashmere trousers (my best trousers) into a tight grey dress that made my ass and waist look great. The dress was completely plain and grey with no embellishments, so it didn't feel like a statement or an attempt at being sexy, but I knew it looked good.

We went back and forth between the bed and the sofa. He would always decide when he'd had enough of talking and would carry me to the bed.

Here, this time, we had our first intimate experience. At least our first semi-sober, memorable experience. We kissed on and off, we rolled around. I had told him I didn't want to fuck.

Last time it didn't click and I knew I was ovulating round about now. So the kissing was good and it got heavy. I let him touch me and I thoroughly enjoyed his hand. It felt like a genuine interaction. I could appreciate it and become excited by it. My body was enjoying it and showing its approval through the communication of hot, sweet wetness. We played around for an hour or so. I told him I was shy with sex and it often took me time to build up to making the first move.

I enjoyed the interaction. I washed my face and brushed my teeth before returning to sleep for the night.

We fitted very comfortably side by side. However we were delicate to each other's movements. When he turned I turned too, and my head always found a corner to tuck itself into—a shoulder or a hand. I believe we managed to sleep the entire night holding each other.

I slept well. It wasn't a drunken sleep. It was kind and soft. I woke up shortly after 07:00. I believe my body was still enjoying the clock change, so I awoke at a modest time. I could have laid in bed until past 09:00, but I felt restless. I drank a glass of water and looked at my face in the bathroom mirror. My skin seemed relatively smooth. I knew I would be lounging around for a couple of hours in the house, so I put on my lilac pyjamas and didn't bother with my hair or makeup. My hair always looked amazing the morning after. All of the rolling around emphasised my curls. My hair naturally fell into the same soft waves each day. It looked like something I would have spent hours crafting with hot rollers a couple of years before. Maybe I had just forgotten how beautiful my hair looked when long.

I sat on the sofa writing and listening to the radio. I drank the remaining half a glass of vodka and coke.

It is approaching 09:00 and I don't know how long VF sleeps in for. I imagine he can sleep all day. Men just seem to have this unspoken power, they can sleep and sleep.

I felt extremely comfortable, as I had imagined it, early in the morning, writing on his couch. The house was warm. I wondered if he had done that intentionally, so that I would always walk around in minimal clothing.

I was facing my bags. I had my day-to-day bag, my writing bag and then a bag of clothing. A pair of shoes, a pair of trainers and my coat sat beside my bags, half on the wooden floor and half on a modest pastel coloured Persian rug. I hadn't noticed the rug last time. It was a great touch and completed the room. It was gentle on the eye, it complimented the walls and grey couch immensely. Small touches. Very good.

It is approaching 10:00 and I am growing increasingly keen to start my day. I think the best way to do so would be to squeeze back into bed next to VF for half an hour so as to gently wake him. I don't feel like intimacy apart from hand-holding. I would like to shower, drink coffee, eat a pastry and go out exploring and continue the conversation. Today I should like to record one of our conversations on my handheld recorder.

I went back to bed for an hour, made messy morning love and slept a little longer. The day was opening up beautifully. I decided to get myself ready to prompt him to do so too.

He slept a little longer. I chose to explore the local streets on foot. I thought I may even indulge myself in a cup of coffee out. VF had one of those charming Italian Moka coffee makers. You had to light the hob with a match and leave the coffee and the steam and the water to do their thing for five minutes or so. Another of VF's small charms. I didn't know how to use it though.

I walked up the familiar street of Ladbroke Grove, not sure what I was hoping to find. However, one of my greatest pleasures emerged right in front of me. I didn't notice it until I was almost past it.

'THE FLOWER CORNER'

This wasn't an ordinary florist or stall—there were rows of the most extraordinarily unusual flowers. October is a random time for flowers, but there was the most fantastic array; Celosias, Dahlias, Chrysanthemums, Nerines, Begonias.

Here I was, fuckin' Mrs Dalloway. I was here and doing it. I had nothing but time, a man waiting for me at home, and a crumpled fiver in my pocket that I had found down the crack of VF's sofa this morning. What could a fiver get me in West London? I couldn't think of anything better for me to return home with than a bunch of something beautiful and seasonal. I spent a couple of minutes fingering buds and leaves. They were all awfully overpriced, mostly a fiver per stem. Returning home with one stem seemed like some hugely romantic gesture so I decided I needed a bunch of something cheap. I strolled up and down the narrow walkway of flowers looking up at me. I became frustrated and nearly settled on some Jerusalem Artichoke stems. The faded greens and purples would nicely enhance the subtle tones of the rug in the living room. I bent down to pick them out, when a bunch of Astilbe called to me. They were tucked in a bucket behind the more extravagant buds, yet their silver tones bounced and reflected the light from their surroundings. Astilbe was a subtle plant. Its colours only shone in the right light. She was wispy yet not delicate. She held herself. Three stems were enough to make a statement. The pinks and silvers of her tips completely encapsulated the mood of that late October morning. Delicate worth.

The foreign plant hanging out of the bucket held no label detailing its price or name. I took the three stems and went indoors to two badly dressed middle aged ladies. They snatched the bunch and twiddled it up in brown paper. I barely had time to ask:

"What are these called?"

"Astilbe. Five pounds."

"A-still-bee?"

"Astilbe."

"Great."

My five pound note, spent in the most perfect way. The walk home excited me, the thought of it. Strolling down Notting Hill, my Astilbe in arm, back to a lovely man waiting at the window. I had no desire to explore the streets any more. I headed back home. The morning couldn't get any better. Mrs fuckin' Dalloway.

VF was waiting at the window as I had anticipated. He was getting ready for us to leave. He didn't comment on the flowers. I put them in water in the bedroom.

Hampstead Heath

VF had said I was a human kitten. I pranced around and played, curled up to sleep and everything that I did was:

"LIVING POETRY"

Gross.

He comes out with so many good lines. I was embarrassed to write that last one though. Today I would like to switch the microphone on and capture an entire conversation which I could then type up. You get the idea of the nature of his language, but it is really spectacular in action.

For today, Monday, we had spoken about eating pastries at home before heading to either Hampstead Heath or Richmond for a walk. I adored Richmond. It was my favourite part of London I had explored so far, and the deer would be out. I hadn't knowingly been to Hampstead Heath, so I was feeling more inclined to head that direction.

Whilst discussing our plans for the day I had wondered how his interactions with me would change in public—whether he would call me babe and squeeze my arm in a coffee shop, and such. I confronted the topic straight away, laying in bed. I didn't have the patience to wait and see.

"How will you act with me in public? What will the dynamic be?"

"I'm surprised you're asking me this. You're the new generation, the snowflakes. Surely you know that nobody cares about this stuff anymore, it's irrelevant."

"I mean, will you snog me in public?"

"What, you want me to? I mean sure. You're a very lovely young lady and I'm a lovely older guy; we are both in demand, but we are together, and that's it. I'll kiss you, yeah, but you want everyone to see? We may have to snog for half an hour for anyone in Hampstead to walk past and notice, so for maximum effect we should just head to Oxford Street."

"You know what I mean."

Fucking cunt. I should have known to expect an answer like that. He sounds like a Richard Curtis film half the time. I bet he thinks that he is a poor man's Hugh Grant.

I was worried about how I would feel the first morning upon arrival. I was worried I would be desperate to flee and on the first train home. But I am superbly comfortable. I am on the sofa doing my writing and VF is sound asleep and everything feels great. I am not feeling so manic with energy but instead awfully relaxed and at home. I'll even have a shower and a cigarette or two soon. It's heavenly; two people with no commitments. Nothing but time and a modest little home.

My mind keeps wandering to long term propositions. Last night in bed I had almost asked him if he'd like to be my boyfriend, just for the reaction mostly. I had imagined what paintings I would bring to hang on each wall. The picture in his bathroom I mentioned earlier was my favourite. I love people who take the time to decorate the bathroom. All rooms should depict an aspect of you.

I took a break for a cigarette. I was still lounging in my pyjamas. It was extremely cold and bitter. Summer had truly faded for good. The heating had not yet come on. The sofa conveniently faced the bedroom door. The blinds were open and the room light and comforting. VF had still not moved from his slumber. I went back to writing for another hour.

I will shower and eat in an hour, before we start our day. When it is this cold it feels like the day needs more planning, but these days are often the best.

As I said, I could imagine myself growing very comfortable here. I was listening to the same music that I listened to in previous houses.

Hopping from house to house didn't feel so appealing when it was this comfortable here. I had every convenience here and the biggest underground network of trains at my doorstep. London truly is spectacular. In DM's home there was a decorative jug in the bathroom that said:

'When man is tired of London, he is tired of life.'

It was cheap but cute. It had stuck with me, therefore it was good.

I imagined how I would choose to decorate. A shoe rack with one tier for mine and one for his. I wonder what he would wear today. I had only seen him on three different occasions. He dressed simply, like me. Today I would have to dress warmly and for the entire day. I would wear my best trousers, a knitted blouse, black cardigan and my dress shoes. I could leave two of my bags here and just take my day bag.

I wonder if we will take photos of each other out and about. I wondered if he would get up and work on his laptop parallel to me. This thought swung me back to a memory of DM and I. Lying on opposite sofas, reading our own books, occasionally looking up to acknowledge each other with a sly smile, topping up each other's glass. A kind afternoon that was, when the summer heatwave was coming to an end and I never thought he would leave.

I am getting bored now. Still no movement from VF. He said he would get a phone call at 06:00 which would mean he had to work. If he didn't get a phone call it was a good (but unpaid) day. The only work I knew of him having lined up involved him going to France on Thursday, and coming back Friday night.

I didn't have plans beyond today, but maybe I would stay until Thursday. I'm not sure he trusted me enough to stay there alone—I'm not sure I would want to—but I think ultimately he did trust me. He joked about me stealing from him. All I'd stolen was a passport photo from his wallet. Sure, I'd had a rummage and a look around but that was out of curiosity. There was nothing of worth that he could steal from me—I kept my jewellery at home in my box. I didn't wear jewellery out. I felt like I didn't need further embellishment but it was nice to have a couple of prized possessions in a box that I could go to on a rainy day. I would end up selling them on a rainy day, no doubt.

I had been thinking of selling the art deco engagement ring from NB. Bless her. I had no idea what was going on there. She had a way with words like VF, but she embellished things more. She wasn't so much a storyteller, but she had great wit. I really would have stopped by her home on many occasions in the last few months, but she insisted she did not want company. We could meet on her terms when she was ready, which was fine.

The ring had no purpose to serve me. I never took it out to admire it or dwell on what it was at the time. We were both searching for something, anything, and took the best thing that came despite it not being the perfect set up. We laughed a lot. She was similar to VF in this respect. We had the same dynamic. I was obsessed with listening to her talk. I didn't care so much for the physical aspect, it happened a good couple of times, but it wasn't a defining feature of the relationship—nor was it with me generally, in any of the meaningful interactions throughout my lifetime.

It is amazing be able to document one day in such detail. However, when you stop to reflect, you realise it is more about how the interactions take you to a past memory, rather than the interactions themselves. The older I get and the more experiences I gather, the longer it will take me to tell the actual story. I notice this in day to day conversation and I have to stop myself from interrupting other peoples' stories. A line of thought, a place, a person, a song or a scent so easily triggers a flashback to a memorable experience that I feel the need to share.

I wonder if this is the motivation behind my diaries—this constant desire to share.

There is not a lot I feel the need to hide. I love being up front. I love raw, brutal honesty. I love watching shock. I love seeing others' admiration of a different attitude. My stories are in no way unique, as they are based on human experiences shared between myself and another existing person. You can read their experience of the story too. I always just felt I had to document, be it through photographs, scrapbooks or receipts. It was not a compulsive obsession, I just took huge delight in reflecting upon past experiences in a form or medium that was stronger than thought alone.

Personally, I find it distasteful to make memories over the phone. I try to avoid using phones when my mental stability is lacking. Depression and mania can too easily trigger artificial feelings that are not sincere. I will not talk about the phone much here.

I have now spent two hours writing and I am considering returning to bed to cuddle for an hour or so. However, I think VF should get up and acknowledge me writing before 10:00.

It has been a great morning and I should like to write this way every morning. It is hard to document a full day's happenings between the morning and noon—during the writing process there may be new advancements.

This is why I am sometimes reluctant to start the writing process. There is too much to cover and ordering it all can be overwhelming. I decided a long time ago that mess is better than no substance at all, so, whatever it is, it gets written down.

Options

I had written to DM three times so he knew of my plans to be in London. His place of work (if he hadn't lost his job) was one mile (or a 22 minutes' walk) away. So tempting. A walk away, just to White City. It was incredible luck.

He finished work at 17:30. I could very easily hang around outside, smoking and reading whilst waiting for him. I hadn't made up a story yet. I hadn't even thought of it until now. Why was I residing one mile from his place of work? What magical force had brought me here? I was sat on a couch one mile from his desk. I didn't know what his work building looked like. I could have ventured out to see him on his way this morning, but nobody needs that kind of interruption at 09:00 on a Monday, in winter. Perhaps if we were still in the heatwave then I would have.

So I have decided to show up at his work promptly for 17:20. I will leave VF's by 16:30 if I am to walk, and draw a map of directions by hand. I hate using my phone in public.

I don't know what will await me—a bitter man or a man with open arms. I don't know how long it will last—a brief ten minutes of conversation, or drinking deep into the night. I cannot predict.

Anyway. He had ignored all of my calls, despite my telling him I was in London. I assume the letters had arrived and he had opened them. I don't believe he had the willpower not to do so. I decided he must know and was not objecting to me turning up. I hoped he might find it romantic and flattering to have me materialise and be waiting for him patiently.

He might emerge with a group of colleagues and ignore me. He might not be there. He might be away. He might watch me from the window and laugh, work overtime, and wait for me to grow tired and cold and leave. I sincerely hope that won't happen.

I had a couple of choices of days to commence this mission. There was no rush today. I didn't particularly feel like doing it today anyway. I was hoping VF and I would enjoy such a lovely day I would struggle to find time to even consider this plan. It was an option, I'd keep it in mind.

The second option is a handsome older economic journalist. He also tried his hand at writing. I believe we could have a lot of fun together, if the conversation flowed. I wasn't interested in any romantic or sexual connections. I just wanted to line up a Plan B if VF failed me.

This man worked in the City and had dropped two names of places we could meet. I liked that—taking a good lead and showing aspects of your personality too, the places you like to be and be seen. He had suggested a Mexican cocktail bar in Soho that looked like fun. It was decorated as a sex shop on the outside. We could meet at 18:00 and go from there. It was an option. Get dinner and drinks on him, before returning to VF. I had told VF briefly last night this was my plan; I would be out in Soho but not home too late. He laughed and wasn't surprised, but I could sense his disappointment I wouldn't be around for the next few days.

Again, this was just an option. I didn't have to do anything I didn't feel up to. I would take the day as it came. However I would keep my phone charged and my options open.

I was hoping Mr Economist would have a nice home I could use as a base to write from sometimes, so he could feed and entertain me too.

Plan C. Ladbroke Grove man. I knew little of him apart from the fact he lived up the road. I shared the address with VF and he confirmed it was nearby. We named him 'my other Ladbroke Grove man'. It was convenient; he looked fun and playful. I wasn't overly keen, but yeah, an option.

<u>Dizzy in a haze for six days</u>

VF and I finally got our act together. I was conscious the daylight was slipping away. We spent a lot of time sleeping or fucking. We rarely slept off our hangovers before mid-afternoon. We hadn't eaten but made time to shower. We both put on our winter coats and left. VF was wearing a gorgeous deep warm brown coat with a black cashmere scarf, which he later left on the underground.

We took the overground from Shepherd's Bush to Hampstead Heath. I was looking forward to being together in public. It had been almost two weeks since the first time we had left the house together—that first meeting outside the pub.

We walked slowly towards the train, chatting most of the way. I felt drained. Our conversation didn't flow as well when we were walking. I was too self-conscious and busy admiring the surroundings—the houses, the people, the cats. We stopped to pet a cat for a couple of minutes. It is always comforting to see somebody else stop to pet a cat. It's like we're on the same wavelength. The train was almost empty bar a strong Irish accent to the left. Nobody looked at us. Heads kept down. VF's posh English voice always dominated everyone else's. I liked watching this in action, in public. I enjoyed his boldness.

VF was too preoccupied to realise he had left his scarf on the train. He only noticed as we left the station. I am still baffled by how his mind operates. It appears to be very systematic and grounded in routine; it seems structured. I am not concerned, but he is quite chaotic at times.

A black cashmere scarf. Luxurious yet straightforward.

There was a street of shops and a small vegetable stand. I hinted we should buy a pumpkin for later on. Halloween was round the corner.

We called into a bakery across the street to grab something to eat. We never really discussed our next plan. One of us just walked in one direction and that was it. So he strolled into the bakery and I followed. He decided he didn't fancy a £5 ciabatta, or whatever, and walked to the chicken shop next door. I had spotted a Daunt Bookshop a couple of doors down. I retained a pleasant memory of a morning in the Daunt store in Marylebone with DM just a few months ago.

He appeared by my side ripping into a piece of chicken. I went in for a bite but it was a side of the wing he had already had a good go at and the meat looked nasty and grey. I decided against it.

We walked up the street towards the Heath. VF said he used to live here but the area had become increasingly expensive and he watched French people buying the houses we couldn't afford anymore. He also told a story of a teenage party he had crashed here where a trustafarian kid screamed at him:

"BLOOD CLART"

We arrived at the Heath. Winter had truly arrived, she was bitter cold, devastatingly so, it made every nerve ending tingle. I constantly tapped my nose with my mitten to make sure it wasn't dripping. This produced a red nose the entire day, but it was fine, we were just walking. Or at least it was fine until he pulled a fucking camera out.

I had seen online he had different albums of photographic portraits. Some of them were stunning. I kept this in mind, although 21 years of experience told me I did not have a photogenic face. I wasn't going to fool myself. I was pretty only in particularly warm light and from a certain angle (slightly to the left). I decided to refuse to have my photo taken as it would save us both the embarrassment of looking back at it later. But he was insistent. I thought of the photos of his I'd seen and liked, and persuaded myself to give it a playful go. It seemed more vanity to refuse a photograph, than to allow one to be taken. I had also told myself this was a great backdrop; nature at her finest. Sure, this could work.

The Heath was gorgeous. At one place you could see over London—the city part with skyscrapers. It reminded me of a scene in the film *Somers Town*. I wanted to relive that film but VF walked the opposite direction, away from the vista and into the greenery. I suppose this spoke a lot of his personality. I followed him and we walked. He had ditched the chicken box in someone's bin.

Now it is just him in his charming brown coat, and the monstrous camera.

I have decided to skip a part of the story as it makes more sense to tell it now.

I perused the photos once we had returned home, they were better than anything I could have imagined. Nobody had ever captured me in the way I had wanted to be captured, but he had succeeded. I now knew that it was everybody else's failing, rather than the aesthetics of my face. He had done it. I finally looked good in a photo. Two photos in particular struck me because I looked so shy and reserved. I looked timid, as I had felt at the time, but I looked beautiful. This small detail of our interaction enhanced my feelings for him. He knew how I wanted to be perceived. Perhaps he was really more interested in the light, the backdrop, or whatever, but he had captured me as a human more accurately than anyone else had in 21 years.

We pursued our afternoon on the Heath. We exchanged few words and walked at different speeds. Sometimes I was in front and sometimes behind. It didn't matter, we were walking. We stopped to smoke a cigarette, we stopped to kiss and we stopped to take a couple of photographs. I was still reticent in front of camera, but I allowed it to happen. The walk lasted several hours. I was beginning to feel drained but a stop off at a 15th century pub kicked me back into action. A double vodka before the walk home.

We downed our drinks fast; we needed them. I paid.

The walk continued via Hampstead to the underground home. It was dark and the day was growing colder. I was aware of how cold my face was. Every part of my face felt as if it had been extinguished after being on fire all day. We hopped on the train and I buried my face into his rib cage. My head was the same height as his chest, so I drooped into it naturally. I can't remember what my legs were doing, no doubt they were entwined with his. The train was full and overcrowded so we were forced to stand together. Nobody cared and nobody looked. As the stations passed the train grew emptier. We remained nestled into one another. My mind fluttered back to the conversation that we had had the previous morning.

"Will you snog me in public?"

I tried my luck, I got my snog.

I peered at the people around us from time to time. Nobody gave a fuck, VF was right. Nobody looked, nobody had any interest in me, or him, or us. All was well. Maybe I wished they were interested. Maybe I would have enjoyed the attention. Maybe that is why I looked at them. I closed my eyes.

We called by the grocery store as we continued our journey home.

Milk
Eggs
Vodka
Coca Cola
Dark chocolate
Grapefruit (I wanted pink but they only had white)

The evening was a blur. We carried on with the vodka. He sometimes drank JD and I sometimes drank wine, but vodka was always reliable. Vodka never gave me a hangover and it never upset my stomach. Vodka is always reliable.

More London floating

We often slept late. I would wake up early but find myself back in bed before long. There is nothing better than spooning in bed with a man twice your size.

I would make coffee and breakfast. Breakfast mostly consisted of a variation of bread and eggs—french toast, poached or scrambled eggs on toast, whatever. Eggs and bread were easy and kept you going for half of the day. I liked to buy fresh fruit if I had money.

The first act of the morning was to gather our receptacles from the night before. We would switch between glasses and mugs, so I would wash them in preparation for the day ahead.

We would function for a couple of hours when we woke up, performing small chores like the dishes, bathing, checking emails for work, and listening to the radio. We didn't tend to drink until it got dark. I was never much of one for alcohol. Three drinks was my limit.

Tuesday held no plans; we hadn't discussed anything. The day started late. It was bitter and dark so I felt no pressure to awake early. I tossed and turned in bed for a couple of hours until mid-afternoon.

It was at the back of my mind. I kept trying to push it away but it kept coming back up. I mean sure, it wouldn't hurt, would it? I decided I had to give it a go. I wouldn't know how long I would be in London, I had to go and see DM.

I had done my research. I made a small paper map of the walk. Head left to Shepherd's Bush, head west, cut down to White City. It was that easy, just down the road. Once I had arrived I realised I could see his office building from the house. All this time, I had been just down the road. Of course, we wouldn't have it any other way.

I arrived with lots of time to waste. It was too cold to wander the streets for longer than I had to. I found Shepherd's Bush library on the walk and I decided I could spend an hour reading whilst 17:00 crept up.

I felt delirious the entire hour. My mind was hyper and wandering. I had not the slightest idea what the evening would bring. The coldest of realities was that I would be waiting outdoors in the cold in a corner of a foreign town for a man that didn't want me, only to walk home alone. I didn't for a moment consider that to be an option. Surely he would welcome me with open arms? I was hopeful.

I had written to him several times over the course of the approaching weeks. I hadn't received a response. I didn't care, I knew he still cared for me nonetheless. He wanted to drag out the romance by playing it cold. I would turn up and we would have a grand reunion—he would take me out for a warm bowl of ramen and we would enjoy a night of passion, then leave it for a couple of weeks and repeat.

The last time we met had been one of those last-minute nights of passion. It was a glorious night. We had sex in the garden. He left for work in the morning and I had returned home. I mostly couldn't wait to see his reaction when I told him I was here. I was in London, I was making a home of it. Ha.

I found myself unable to focus in the library. I flicked a couple of pages of a book (with a forgettable title) then decided to write another letter to DM. I hadn't posted the letter I wrote on Monday so I could just put them in the same envelope.

The building had an escalator that ran straight through the middle. It was glass. I could watch everyone, every single worker to-ing and fro-ing from the office and the street. It was a spectacular sight, witnessing everyone doing their thing. I counted the floors and located the sixth, where he worked. I watched and watched the hordes of people in the elevator. At last, at 17:40 I saw him enter the glass box and ride downwards. I didn't see him acknowledge or even catch a glimpse of me, he just hurriedly turned a corner and disappeared. I continued to wait. 15 minutes and nothing. Well, I suppose there must have been a side door. I had ran out of luck and retired to VF's house.

It was the coldest day of the year so far. Every movement was painful. I couldn't face the 20 minute walk in this cold. I boarded the train at White City and made my way back to Ladbroke Grove.

My evening appeared desolate. I had no plans. VF was playing football in the evening but would return later on. I didn't know if he would be home when I arrived. I scrolled my phone in a quest for a back up plan.

Renaissance man of Ladbroke Grove. We had spoken briefly for a week or so. He lived a couple of roads away. I decided it might be worth a shot. He was close enough for it to not be a big commitment or disappointment if it didn't go well.

I let myself into VF's house. He was getting ready to leave for football. I had to make a quick turnaround. I powdered my nose and put on lipstick.

"Oh, you're not staying?"

"I just had to use the bathroom. I'm back out again now. I'll be home in a couple of hours, I'll see you then."

I made my way swiftly through the cold to the pub on the corner of the street. The same pub where I had met VF. It was a safe bet. I knew my surroundings and the atmosphere would be fine. We agreed to meet in ten minutes' time. Ideal.

I rocked up and he was nowhere to be seen. I bristled at the thought of buying my own drink (not because I'm a woman but because he no doubt had more money than me). I assumed my money was running out but I was too busy and ignorant to check. I considered waiting outside for him to arrive and buy the drinks but it was too cold. I bought myself a double vodka and orange juice.

It was relatively quiet here. There were a lot of older men on their own, watching me, watching me waiting. I perched in a corner, eyeing up another older man at the bar. This went on for a couple of minutes, then he arrived.

I hadn't thought through a game plan, I simply knew that I was feeling rubbish and so I just wanted to have some fun to distract my mind from the thoughts of today's disaster in White City.

Vomit dress in a bag

We got on just fine. I can't remember what he did for a living but we had a couple of drinks at the pub before he invited me to a dinner party. It wasn't far away, so I went along as his guest.

It was weird. Around ten women in their late twenties and three men in their late forties. The host poured me champagne and I spoke about my diaries. I drank and ate chicken with salad. There was a BBQ on the balcony and I think there was seafood on it too.

I turned on my handheld recorder and kept it in my pocket so I could record the conversations. They weren't anything special. A waste of battery.

I over-ate and over-drank, topped off with a chocolate cake made with hash (or something). Next thing I'm on the balcony holding in my vomit, until it sprays through my hands everywhere. A total embarrassment. I didn't care to impress anyone. I'd had my fun.

My date walked me home, carrying my vomit-stained dress in a Tesco bag. I apologised but he didn't seem to mind. VF took me inside and put my vomit dress in the washing machine while I retired to bed. Maybe I am not made for London. A few days in and I can't handle myself.

To do list

- Update diaries
- Think about why I like VF
- Clean VF's house
- Decide if I want to be a lover or muse (half-joke)

VF is standing on the tube as I sit down to write this.

<u>Moving in</u>

Weeks had passed. Delusional weeks. To and fro. I'm sorry for not writing. I don't write so much when I am happy.

VF and I were too busy with a blossoming romance to notice the changes in the weather, the festivities, or our slipping sanity. Brexit was unfolding around me. I barely noticed the details, the madness, the pleas, the weirdness.

Everyone else seemed very angry. It was mayhem. I was busy rearranging VF's furniture whilst he was at a funeral somewhere up north.

I walked down to Notting Hill Gate and browsed the charity shops although I had no money to spend. I bought a copy of Capote's short stories and went to the photo shop to print a small photo of VF and I. I Blu-tacked the photo of us next to his desk and read for the rest of the day.

I made a savoury tart of cranberry and cheese for dinner and left it in the fridge for when he gets home.

The Christmas season

I had barely noticed the festive season was approaching. We were too caught up in our romance. The train journey, a once tedious, long journey now seemed comforting and pleasant. It was a trip I undertook twice a week, on the way to see the one, the love, my warm buzz.

For the first time, I had started to question our habits.

On this train I struggle to write. Nowhere makes me write as well as when I'm perched at VF's desk, waiting at the window for him to come home. Nowhere works as well. My muse. He's my fucking muse.

I understand now the difference between being a muse and being in love. VF had fuelled the writer in me that had previously been left to rot. Something DM and the rest had not cherished.

'Love is the druuuuuug and I neeeeed to score'

I liked this idea and the actual reality of me writing on a train and drinking on a train, the old people around me shit scared of this young woman swigging from a bottle and writing furiously for the next hour. They knew that she was a force to be reckoned with. They left her to it.

The best part of the train journey is having a cigarette at King's Cross before I make my change. The reward after the uncomfortable journey. The reward for being me, for having freedom, for somehow finding myself in the capital, the coolest city in the world, for being 21, for having little money to play with, for having nothing to spend but time. The best time to be alive and the best place to be. The cigarette at the train station.

The cigarette is a dying fashion. We got over killing ourselves and suddenly everyone wants to live longer. People should avoid horse riding if they want to live longer. I'm not bothered about my current state of existence because I am currently too indulgent.

Messages from JD (Seattle boy)

I have never met him but we have spoken online for six years.

"It's infuriating that people I know, know you somehow.
I doubt they know who you are to me."

"They like my stuff?"

"They follow your stuff!"

"You like my stuff?"

"Why are they doing that? You are like a secret love I keep hidden away."

"Well declare the love. People who follow me love my real life drama, it's their favourite part of my diaries. Let's add another layer to the story then."

"Let's think about doing something."

"I'm writing full time now and I live with a man."

"Jealous of that man. I'm handsomer than he."

"But this one has so much wit it makes it easy to write."

Paris

On my journey between London and the Fens I had to change trains at King's Cross. I had to turn right. The trains to the left were the trains to Paris. I always hoped one day I would turn left. Before long, I was.

We spent Christmas day together drinking champagne and eating an array of meats in matching Santa hats. VF bought tickets for the train to Paris. I think I screamed for the next three weeks in excitement. I had never been to Paris.

On the train we listened to Françoise Hardy, Jacques Dutronc, France Gall and the rest. We finished a bottle of fizz and the night went a little fuzzy.

I found an AirBnB in République (which I now know is not the safest part of Paris, but still pleasant).

First we went to a cafe where we drank red wine and smoked Gauloises. They were too strong for me but I had wanted to buy them at the train station just to try.

VF had lived in Paris and studied at The Sorbonne in the early nineties. He showed me around Paris, from the Latin Quarter to the tip of the right bank. It was as spectacular as I had always imagined. A city moulded by a single man. A vision.

It snowed. I drank mulled wine and popped codeine to warm myself up.

I climbed the Eiffel Tower on foot and on drugs.

He introduced me to a Parisian friend, whom I immediately hated. She obviously took a lot of cocaine. She disliked me immediately too. She told me she didn't want me to date VF. We had an uncomfortable dinner and went home. It was the only time we ate out in Paris. VF said he'd rather save the money, which upset me. I would have paid my own way, but he found restaurants a hassle and being waited on an uncomfortable experience.

There was snow in England when we landed. By the time we reached VF's it was past midnight. The keyhole in the front door had frozen over with ice we had to poke through. I was so cold I thought I would be cold for years to come. Not even a hot bath or cuddles cured it. I was cold for days.

Choose a club

I was beginning to grow worried about VF and I. I had thoughts along the lines of 'what do I do when he dies?' I'll run out of lines. When I'm with him the diaries just write themselves. Maybe I'd just document the entire romance, properly, from the beginning, and in detail.

I tried not to think so horridly.

He was out drinking with a friend and would be home by midnight. I wasn't feeling overwhelmingly in love, but I felt positive. I had no money. It would be a couple of poor, drunken days. I had a bottle of red and two packs of cigarettes, two outfits, two magazines and Capote's short stories. That was plenty of content for the coming week. Another week dedicated to VF. Wonderful.

Fuck the laundry back home. I'm better off here any day. The train back to London, Sunday night, 21, aren't I lucky and aren't you jealous?

Once aboard the train back to his I appeared to have forgotten all my prior worries about VF. Some days we just lived an idyllic existence side by side and I didn't feel like I had to worry. I wasn't worrying about my own existence right now either. The worries I had before about being a 'Fen girl' or a 'London girl' had vanished. I was existing as both simultaneously, quite calmly and successfully. I didn't have to commit to either club.

I don't want to blame the change in seasons, but getting trains in the daylight definitely helped, despite ultimately being a winter person.

I dropped a line to my grandad and grandma, catching up on my granddaughterly duties. My grandad lived on a ranch in

Colorado, USA. He had come to visit me in England last Autumn but he still felt very mysterious and unknown to me, even though he is my blood.

I should like to take a trip to visit him in the summer—my first solo USA trip. VF and I had spoken about buying a car to drive across the USA, starting on the east coast and heading south. We were both obsessed with Ry Cooder and wanted to visit the Louisiana Bayou.

The other week VF took me to the theatre to see a Sam Shepard tribute of short plays, after which we spoke to some of the actors VF knew. Then we went to see *True West* with front row seats! I felt so spoilt and like a princess. The play was amazing. There was this scene with 20 stolen toasters all going off at once, just a metre from my face. It was hysterical.

Sorry, back to the trip. The USA trip felt unlikely, but a sweet thought to keep in mind. It could be possible. I would continue to not touch my money so the option was there, but first we had Cannes. VF had gone every year for the last 15 years, or something ridiculous. If I went it would be in just under two weeks. I was to confirm the details today. After that, dress shopping. Now my hair had grown out from being cropped short I felt a little more beautiful again, like I was in my physical prime (which I estimate to have been at age 16).

A deep red silk cami dress would work perfectly for Cannes.

"Be careful going out like that, you'll be swamped with marriage proposals. You look like a doll. More cosmopolitan."

Cosmopolitan? Did I look like a village girl all bare faced before? This pissed me off. Stupid village girl trying on dresses for Cannes. I shan't go. At Cannes I'd be lost.

Portobello coffee

Monday was a dream, no commitments. I awoke by VF's side and felt obliged to spend the day outside, to get some writing done over coffee and enjoy London. I couldn't think of anywhere I'd rather be. Portobello Road just on my doorstep, drinking a hot chocolate with a bag of lunch-ready vegetables at my side.

Summer had enabled me to sit outside and write. I bought my hot chocolate with espresso and perched on a corner table outside a cafe. The cafes here were unglamorous and rather samey—dirty tables, uncomfortable metal chairs and people approaching you begging for money almost constantly. It made for an interesting backdrop to the writing because there was always something to see.

At last I was happy and felt at home. My London. It beat drinking coffee in the Fens, where nobody spoke to you and there was nothing to watch.

An elderly woman with white hair asked me to reserve the chair next to me whilst she bought a coffee. She looked rough, but not homeless. She carried a floral walking stick and a little green trolley full of groceries. We exchanged polite introductions and she asked about the Fens. She herself had lived on Ladbroke Grove for 40 years. She lived alone and had tried renting rooms to tenants, but ultimately didn't trust them alone in her home. She had filterless pre-rolled cigarettes that she kept in a pouch, simply scrunched at the end and growing soggy as she sucked. She seemed to know everyone on the street—all the street vendors. This was her own little Fens.

A man who was probably homeless joined our table, drinking cider out of a Coca Cola bottle. He told me he would be given a few quid if he helped pack away the stalls. He said he didn't want to beg and that people would always find a job for him.

It seemed an unlikely friendship. He accompanied her to the grocery store carrying her bag, and she rolled him cigarettes. I sat between them whilst they talked over me, and I tried to write, but was too intrigued by their friendship.

The elderly have always depressed me. People should not live that long. To grow older, poorer, less trusting, but still happy to sit by the market and talk to anyone. I don't know. Old people tend to give up as their bodies do.

I finished my chocolate and said goodbye. He replied:

"Goodbye nice lady."

I continued down Portobello Road looking for somewhere else to sit outside. The north side (I assume it's north, or maybe east) was cheaper and less touristy. The opposite end was more 'Instagrammable'.

A pair of Victorian boots in a shop window caught my eye so I went in. Tourists were trying on vintage Burberry coats whilst I sat on a pile of blankets waiting for the lady to get the shoes from the window.

"These boots are very small you know."

"I have ballerina feet. I think they'll fit."

I pulled the boots up, laced them and strolled up and down the shop. They were something I might imagine Betty Page wearing. Black leather, a fetishistic high heel and tight, real tight.

"My God. Nobody has ever managed to get them on. They must be a size two. And it's not just that, they are so narrow, what did you do to your feet to make them fit?"

I was wearing socks too.

"Do your parents have small feet too? Because you're not small in height, but your feet must be tiny."

I continued to walk up and down the shop floor, admiring the boots.

"I must take a photo of you in them to send to the owner. We finally found our Cinderella!"

I laughed and posed for a photo in my fetish boots. I was suddenly the attraction of the whole shop. The girl with the tiny feet. I unlaced them and placed them back in the window display. I had no money.

I headed home. For lunch we had English asparagus, Italian ham, English strawberries and a sweet potato. I would cook for both myself and VF.

Portobello continued

"I want to be your English muffin."

"I want to be your boysenberry jam."

"I want to be your no ordinary jam."

"I want to be your chlamydia test."

"I want to be your rash that doesn't clear up."

"I want to be your neighbourhood rat."

"I want to be your pet eagle that eats the neighbourhood rats."

"I want to be your twice removed second cousin of the environmental office minister than bans eagles like you."

VF and I collapsed in laughter. We wanted to be everything today. Especially silly.

We bought a few more items from the market and flowers. I returned home at 16:00 for my midday snooze.

Booze and banging

Sleep did not come today. I argued the entire night with VF over the phone. He found himself in a state of depression and confusion, unable to communicate with me.

I felt guilty spending time with him when I knew he should be working. At first it was a dream—endless days in bed—but now, six months down the line, this felt like reckless behaviour.

"I care for you so much. I dedicate everything to you. It ruins me to see you so self destructive. This is what keeps me up at night."

"What actually keeps me up at night is the vision of that man's penis pounding your immaculate vagina from behind for half an hour. I am sorry."

"Perhaps I find myself in other men's beds because my boyfriend consistently ignores and embarrasses me. He already knows how it feels to watch one's loved ones abuse themselves, and yet he continues to do so nonetheless. I love you but you're difficult to love."

We had parted on a sour note and I sat awake all night. No amount of intellect could justify his self-abuse. Conflicted. Self-destructive. Just like me. We both had to snap out of it if we stood a chance together. It was time to start my day, regardless of whether we spent time together, or if he continued this streak of nihilism.

Despite not making firm plans I found myself with no option but to leave the Fens and head to London. I wasn't prepared to watch him crumble, and consequently watch us crumble too. It had felt like we were back on track two weeks ago, but nothing was ever constant.

Options were whirling through my mind. He may not even be at home upon my arrival.

I arrived; clothes everywhere, dirty glasses on the floor. I scooped the clothes into a corner and dumped the glasses in the sink.

A friend of VF's was visiting this evening. We had met and exchanged words about my diaries briefly, whilst carol singing at Soho House. If I remember correctly, a few mulled wines in he had asked me about the purpose and intention behind the diaries. It felt like an interrogation. I looked forward to his arrival and to continue the conversation. He was far more interesting and had more to offer than I, having trained as a doctor and psychiatrist. VF joked he was his own personal psychiatrist. This meant our house guest no doubt knew all about our relationship issues, but hopefully he knew about the highs too.

We drank vodka followed by coffee on Ladbroke Grove before returning home to take turns choosing Smiths albums. His choice was *Louder than Bombs,* VF's *The Queen is Dead* and my own their eponymous debut album. Debut albums were always the purest—there was no ego to live up to.

When discussing the diaries it finally dawned on me I was practically there and the ground work was done. All I had to do was figure out the beginning and end. The beginning seemed relatively clear. The ending seemed less clear, but it was fast approaching.

"Baby, we gotta figure out an ending for the diaries."

"Does this mean we have to break up, have a fight, marry each other, or die?"

"I'm not sure."

<u>16 years old</u>

I sat in a taxi office at 23:00.

"Ten minutes for a taxi for Jasmine."

Perhaps I should get a job in a taxi office. It would be straightforward and simple. Easy money, except for when the drunks came in, and I'm sure that would happen often. I don't think I've ever taken a taxi sober.

I'm sure I could handle it. I could talk my way out of anything. This skill had taken me many years to learn but I could stand up for myself and make a joke at the same time. After all, how intimidating could a young girl like me be? It's like VF says:

"You've spent years building an image, but I've sacrificed years building a personality."

Or something along those lines. Don't quote me. Enough about fucking VF.

I awoke from a nap dazed and confused. I could have sworn the qwerty keyboard had been rearranged. I couldn't quite find the letters fast enough and words came out backwards. I was still insistent on continuing with my plan of saying 'yes'.

I had confessed to one of my closest friends, FN, that I sometimes felt bound up in the mindset of a confused 16-year-old. Haunting me years on, I was still overrun with anxieties I had never confronted. Anxieties that were lingering and waiting for me to tell them fuck off.

Fuck off.

I'm no longer in a position to accept and validate depression and anxiety. That is not me, I am not someone who suffers from this, I am not feeling this way because of so-called depression, I am feeling this way because I made a decision to feel how I do. Sure, it's going to take a while to train myself out of a mindset, but that plan is already in the works.

Fuck self-care, fuck taking a bath. I don't want to give in to imaginary feelings. I'd rather go out and have a crazy one night stand and wreck my relationship with the love of my life, then spend the following weeks trying to justify to myself why I did it.

I have to destroy myself to understand myself.

VF blames it on our mattress.

Our bed wasn't big enough and that made him grumpy and resentful—the laws of unintended consequence. I didn't want to spend money on a mattress, I slept brilliantly. VF was twice my size and functioned as a huge teddy bear that watched over me whilst I dozed.

Emotions aside, a storm has been brewing here. Is naming storms a new thing that we do, or have we always done this? 'Storm Hannah' she was called. I'd seen photographs of mini tornadoes in the Fens. I took a brief walk in the late afternoon, rain, dust and all. I was thinking about content for writing, but nothing came to me. I felt I should take more time to read Anaïs Nin and refresh my mind about what had inspired all this. My lovers were as exotic as hers, so what was I lacking? Today the words refused to come. I barely had fluid thoughts let alone feelings. I lacked the urge to even cook a meal today. My stomach was tight and aching but I couldn't be bothered to fix it.

I decided I would hunt through my diary archives to include more content from my previous life. It differed so largely in tone, mostly depending on who it was written for—ex-lovers, friends, self-deprecation. Comparison is good. A whole story. Making the links. This is the beginning after all.

Master misery

I dreamt I was wearing a French maid's outfit with stockings whilst sat on a rubber dinghy floating down the Thames. I was flirting with MPs in blue suits, and making small talk.

I'm rubbing my eyes and returning to sleep for however long I can make it last. I apologise for the lack of content. I need sleep.

Train diaries

I was most productive on early morning trains. The 06:20 King's Cross to Ely gave me a euphoric feeling of self worth and practicality. I could function in the early hours and be a useful member of society. I rubbed shoulders with the workers and holidaymakers on the early morning trains. The only downside was that nowhere was open so I couldn't buy a pot of hot porridge. Instead, I procured a can of Fanta and a family-size bar of dark chocolate to get me through the morning.

I had rolled out of bed wearing the same white silk blouse and jeans I had been wearing most of the week. I borrowed a black cashmere jumper of VF's and wore new ballet pumps. I didn't bother brushing my teeth because it is the worst chore. You may find this disgusting but I just can't bring myself to brush my teeth; not until they feel or taste bad. This will come to haunt me in years to come, but I'll have them whitened when I have money.

I popped a mint and a spray of Halfeti—a blend of sandalwood, tobacco, vanilla and Jasmine. The whole train could bask in my beautiful scent. Perfume was always of huge importance to me. It stimulates the most overlooked sense. I wanted my aroma to create memories, I wanted men to long for the distinct smell of me as I did theirs. I wanted VF to smell me on everything he owned, compelling him to call me when I was away. Today he was working—another court case. At least we were both out of bed before 07:00 and busy trying to make money.

Vroooosh and I emerge from a tunnel somewhere around Finsbury Park. Looking up at the skyscrapers I understand people's lack of amazement when they visit the Fens. Our perception of architecture is dulled. Cities are too full and busy with architectural triumphs so, paradoxically, the structures are taken for granted. I crave a return to the Fens. I will spend a few days in solitude, putting in the groundwork for the next few months. I need to decide whether I will make it to Cannes. I decided I should definitely try to do Cannes, in the spirit of trying to wriggle out of this long depression.

Polanski attended Cannes for the first time around my age, when he snuck in (I just finished reading his autobiography). I could fly out and hitch a ride no doubt, and meet VF somewhere along the way.

I realised in the quieter moments I was seriously neglecting my friends. I had many friendships but little felt as compelling as the motivation VF had brought to me. Was it their fault? No. But nothing is as powerful as romance.

I cherished my friendships, but also felt I needed to shy away from the details of my life. I knew my lifestyle seemed extreme to a lot of my friends—the lack of routine, the mad sleeping patterns, the spontaneity, living between houses and never being free for more than an hour or two. When faced with the reality of my lifestyle I would find myself shying away simply because I didn't want to be counselled. It wasn't because I didn't value other's opinions, it was because only I knew my habits and routine, and it felt unfair for people to intrude and tell me how I felt.

I had a falling out with my closest friend earlier in the week. I call it a falling out because it was the closest thing to a loss of connection we had ever had. She had visited London a couple weeks back and I was in no mood to socialise or even function after a week's worth of fighting with VF. Meeting her at King's Cross I was a bottle and a half in of Pastis, downed with sugar free Red Bull and a handful of painkillers. I tried to socialise, ask questions and show an interest in her life, which I genuinely do have and always will, but the words didn't come because I wasn't ready to talk about my week from hell. We met for breakfast the following morning and we spoke a little more, but again I found myself crippled by the loose ends of conversation and ended up cancelling the rest of the day, which I instead slept away in Notting Hill. I confronted her about her previous silence and we both expressed discontent with our last meeting.

We had been living separate lives in different cities for years, so had naturally drifted apart and into new social rhythms and patterns. Tonight I hoped we would cross paths and reconcile any worries we had about one another. My life needed more than just VF.

I found great comfort in female friends. If anything, I wished I had more. I wanted friendships where we stayed up all night chatting and drinking and doing each other's hair before crashing a party. Fuck, just someone to watch TV with.

The sun reemerges somewhere near Royston and my coffee grows cold. Approaching 08:00. The Stranglers comes on shuffle:

'See a picturesque decay there
Something for all time to tell
See the woman of your dreams there
In a baroque bordello'

I call VF from the train to confirm my plans.

"Baby, just wanted to say I'm in for Cannes."

"I'll see what I can do. See you."

"See you."

I had a silk dress to find.

Manic returns

The last few days had been so full of joy, adventure, lovemaking and tenderness that I hadn't found the time to write. Between all of this I was sleeping close to 16 hours a day, cocooned in duvets beside VF, cosy in Notting Hill.

I felt no guilt about not working or dedicating time to write over the last few days. We were busy enjoying each other and the writing could always happen at a later date. We were completely enraptured with one another. We deserved this.

"I'm going to make you addicted to me, so you don't ever need to stray again."

And so I hoped this is how I would remain for the rest of my life. We were utterly content in each other's company. I was learning to rewire my methods of attaining happiness. Was I finally coming to the end of a five year depression? I was learning what made me happy and I was teaching myself what it was I expected from myself.

I find it hard to reflect on my former ways of life—many lovers and many homes, new adventures—some failed and some useful. There had been many moments I grimace and cringe at on reflection, but for once I was accepting myself. After all, I'm approaching my prime and that is something to be cherished. I should be excited by all these new prospects. Say 'yes' to crashing parties at Cannes and the USA road trip. Say 'yes'.

Changing seasons are a good time to implement change. VF had bought me more flattering, tight-fitting clothes in preparation. I was reluctant, but after all I had a gorgeous body I should be proud of. For years I took pride in being 'modest'. Clothes had previously felt useless. But now, in my prime, entering my early twenties, I should grasp every opportunity to show off.

Baguetti Western

I lay barefoot on the couch in my jeans and silk blouse. It was still light outside and approaching 21:00. My first summer in London. I had spent four days lounging in West London, wearing the same outfit, leaving only to attend a film screening and cocktails with the director, topped up with wine from the corner shop on the way home.

VF had spent the last few days at my side, wearing little blue striped shorts and sandals. We were summer babies now. I felt our closeness, that our bond was stronger than ever—something to be cherished and nurtured. I had faith in my writing and my future. I just had to keep it up and stay disciplined. I was happy to spare myself time to enjoy days off alongside VF, but the writing had become an addictive ritual I felt lost without. I wouldn't be able to look back on these days and recount every detail if I didn't write about it. Every day was noteworthy in my eyes, despite spending 22 hours in bed some days.

I only needed to keep the writing up at this rate and at the end of the year I would be ready to publish. That was the greatest motivation right now. I pondered whether I should include photographs of iconic moments alongside the words. I thought back to the Polanski biography and the documentation of Serge and Jane. I should like to include photographs but I worry VF would object. However, they are my diaries so the vision is mine too. Words are reinforced by photographs. Besides I want everyone to see our beauty side by side.

The question of when to begin this series of diaries was also on my mind. I could start pre-dating VF. I could start as a teenager. There were many options and the tone differs so much between each, but consistency often made writing less interesting, and I wanted to include the bumpiness and the shit storms, the younger naïve Jasmine, the meeting of the two.

We sat in the garden smoking and looking at our new plants. I had planted Lavender and strawberries. It was a little bit too hot. VF wanted to watch a French Western later.

"I'm going to write to Pete Bradshaw the Guardian film critic and try and copyright the phrase 'Baguetti Western."

"Sounds good, baby."

Punting

I had never known a sleep like it. VF and I tossed and turned for 6 hours, wearing ear plugs. Our house guest snored very loudly. I jumped out of bed at 08:00 nonetheless. I wasn't joking about the change of climate—this is officially one of the hottest summers ever recorded. Brilliant.

We drank Champagne on a punt down the river. VF looked so handsome and preppy in a white shirt and his little blue striped shorts. Another punt forced us into a corner and we found ourselves stuck in punt roadblock.

"If this was Nascar you'd be disqualified!"

"If this was Nascar you wouldn't be allowed on the track!"

"If this was Nascar you'd be too ugly to win!"

Punt men were harsh but we were worse. King of the Ouse. Or maybe it was the River Cam, or River Bedford. VF was a student at Cambridge years ago which made him a lifelong member. We strolled university grounds the rest of the afternoon.

I had another three days of planned laziness ahead of me. My bank account seemed infinite—money just wasn't disappearing despite my increasing recklessness. Tomorrow I would buy more clothes suited to this climate. VF has requested short shorts. Our houseguest was to depart tomorrow morning leaving our home in desperate need of a deep clean—the thought thrilled me.

A lazy night in with the love of my life—napping, reading, a bath. Nothing else to report. Too happy to be sat alone writing all evening.

<u>More sticky days</u>

A beautiful deep sleep. I was getting rather good at sleeping solidly through the night, I had been riddled with anxiety and borderline insomnia when younger. In my fourth apartment I lived alone. It was beautiful. 200-years-old with huge wooden framed windows, wooden floors, tall ceilings, a modest kitchen and a pink bathtub. It could have been my dream home. It was, for brief moments. I spent a summer and winter there. Summer was dreadfully warm though winter proved cosy. But the house had a terrible aura, and friends agreed too—nobody could sleep there. I would pass out then wake again, constantly. When my bed failed me I would sleep in the kitchen, dragging the duvet from room to room just hoping to find some peace.

At its worst I would drive to McDonalds at 03:00 or 04:00 and sit for hours until I felt myself dropping off. I'd take a book and drink a juice. The cleaners always asked if I was alright, but I'm sure they knew I was. I was showered and presentable and had driven, I just needed a place to kill time until morning arrived and I could give sleep another try.

Over this time I was excruciatingly busy with studying film, writing film, editing film, learning how to use a camera and just learning how to take care of myself aged 19. I'd rewrite short scripts over and over, contact people to help me film different concepts, and try to find composers to write soundtracks. I had next to no money and what little there was seemed to go towards cleaning products. Cleaning was a never-ending job.

On the last week of the month I would run out of money and eat rice for every meal. But I always had plenty of bleach and laundry detergent.

I cooked often (I never ate out) and always ate at the table, alone. I used the kitchen table to work from and do collages. I have a habit of eating in bed nowadays, which I'm trying to undo.

My mind was just so busy trying to absorb information and everything that was given to me. I wanted to experience it all. One man to the next. Friends galore. Watching and reading constantly. I barely noticed the seasons changing.

Now I wonder if I'm just more observant or perhaps global warming really is hitting us. I cannot remember springs and summers like this, not as a child. The last two years we have been blessed with constant beach BBQs, days spent drinking in dresses on the riverbank, walking home in the light at 22:00. It really was getting warmer.

Today was 25 degrees and I put on my yellow jumpsuit. It was that or my New York Herald Tribune shirt. All of my other summer clothes were still in the washing basket.

I could take a trip to visit VF later on if I felt like it, but I wasn't sure I would. I should give him more time to get back into a routine: working, getting the house in order, figuring out the future. But what was I meant to do until then? Sit alone in my house in the Fens, waiting? This is the problem with relationships. I struggle to find myself NOT obsessed with them. I think of VF constantly, pondering whether he would validate the way I'm spending my time. I don't talk to him constantly—one short phone call every other day when we're not staying together. We had just shared five days. I should enjoy a couple of days to myself. I probably won't see him tomorrow, I don't feel like trains and commuting across London, but if he insisted, I'd come.

On a day like today I wouldn't be worrying about company if I had a car. I'd be deep in the Fens at the abandoned quarry, soaking up the sun and finishing off a book with a vegetarian BBQ crackling away (I do eat meat, I'm just terrified of poisoning myself if I cook it). I had to get rid of the car because I only used it to visit the beach or my parents—both a rare occurrence. Every time I started the car the battery would be dead from idleness.

I chose to walk everywhere because I liked to smoke and listen to music. A car was a luxury I only needed a couple of times a year. So carless and afoot I decide to walk down into town for some breakfast alone.

The day unravels slowly and I find myself overcome with boredom. I crave Holland Park in the sunshine and before I know it I'm on a train headed to VF.

If I have the energy I should like to make dinner for us, to redeem myself after a week of lazy dozing. Lemon garlic linguine with white wine was on my mind.

23:56, the ingredients for linguine still sat in the fridge. Perhaps it was too late to cook. Gin and white wine had made the evening fly between Notting Hill and Holland Park.

VF had a houseguest. He hadn't given much away but he used to be a stockbroker and his favourite colour was pink. He went down to the Electric Cinema in the evening to see a film.

He told me about a back door you could use to sneak in. You just had to make sure that you didn't sit in someone else's reserved seat. What's a Wall Street broker doing sneaking into cinemas? I still knew nothing about him. Whilst he was at the cinema VF and I made love for several hours and forgot about the linguine.

I was still convinced he was the one. A 21st century Serge and Jane, living in a one bedroom flat in West London. Too bad I cannot act and he cannot sing.

Time on my hands

The weekend had arrived, but days of the week had little or no relevance to me, the only difference was I might have to queue longer for a cup of coffee.

It felt like a burden to write today, but I knew I owed it to my future self, and dedicated some time in the evening to do so.

I was drowsy in the heat—it had taken over me. I couldn't get comfortable in any chair. I felt the best place for me was bed.

I was barely reading, or watching TV, I was mostly daydreaming and cooking very slowly and eating very slowly. Life was not a rush. This was something I was learning to acknowledge and cherish—I didn't have to be busy to be successful. Being busy gave me a rush; I loved dashing from train to train, meeting to meeting, collapsing into bed in the early hours and waking early to do it all over again. But then I learnt to take more pleasure in doing things slowly. With time one could appreciate small actions—the rituals of bathing, changing laundry (sorry, laundry again).

On reflection, I had spent a lot of time waiting, and therefore had become quite accustomed to having time on my hands. I knew how to make it pass.

Two instances come to mind.

1. The barber shop.

When I was a young girl my mother worked an office job on Thursdays and maybe one other day over the weekend, I believe it was Sundays. It must have been, because my dad would take me out for a roast dinner in King's Lynn on Sundays.

On Thursdays I would wait for my father to finish work, for I wasn't allowed to be alone at the house after school. I would sit patiently in his barber shop for a couple of hours until he finished work.

I tried to be entrepreneurial, suggesting I could have my own tiny cash register and take money for haircuts. This idea didn't quite catch on. Instead I would sweep the hair and clean the sinks in exchange for £5. When there was nothing to do I would read newspapers and magazines, gaze out the window and listen in on conversations.

These Thursdays felt long for a young girl, but they also provided an insight into an adult world where I could be a fly on the wall, absorbing conversation and seeing how men spoke to other men.

2. Waiting for the bus.

After my parents divorced my mother moved to a small village miles from anywhere. I had to commute to Cambridge for sixth form college aged 16-17 via bus every day. There was only one bus in each direction.

07:20 and 18:10.

My college classes finished at 15:00 or 16:00 so every day I found myself with hours to kill. I met many characters in the library on these afternoons. Most days it was too cold to wait outdoors. A painter once painted my portrait. A Russian professor tried to buy me. Junkies would pester me for cigarettes. All in the library.

I could buy cigarettes in Cambridge. I would purposely leave my backpack outside the store and walk in with my tight pencil skirt, small-heeled brogues and a folder of some sort.

The street was surrounded by office blocks so I blended in as another office drone.

I was delighted to have mastered this. I received £10 for lunch each week which would buy one pack of 20 cigarettes.

Perhaps waiting for the bus is what led to my smoking addiction—my 17-year-old self's answer to boredom. I'd revise Economics, Politics, English & Religious Studies in the library until they closed at 18:00 then wait outside for the bus.

I became very good at waiting. VF always complained when a London tube was more than three minutes late but rural life means happily waiting half an hour for a train.

I had adapted, like an animal. Now I hated waiting for trains.

I would head back to London on Monday. VF still had guests and the house felt too cramped, so I would stay alone for a couple of days at my parents.

I had no plans for the week, which was how I liked it. We still had to make a trip to Italy to visit his mother. Everything felt at once or not at all. Today was an empty day.

I took a walk early evening hoping to bump into someone I knew so we might exchange words and smoke in the sun. I didn't have the phone numbers of many of my Fenland friends—I just looked for them in the usual places and they either emerged or didn't. Nobody was around today, so I settled down in the sunshine alone with a can of sparkling wine and The Doors. I decided to phone VF. He said I should keep busy with writing short stories. I asked for a subject, he told me:

"Weasel in the gutter."

<u>Weasel in the gutter</u>

I cannot write fiction.

It's approaching 21:00 and I literally laugh out loud at the ridiculousness of myself.

I take my clothes off and turn on the TV. Maybe I'll revisit the weasel tomorrow.

I sink into the TV.

<u>Whatever I say I am</u>

The first. Must you have a first before you are? Was I not a writer until I published a book? Was the justification of writing daily enough to fuel a real writer's ego, or must it be available to buy with pounds sterling via Amazon? All tricky questions but I'd already made up my mind. I had been told again and again I was a writer and had always been a writer. I didn't need justification.

My train journey was bumpy. This train driver must have been in training, or speeding, or the track was fucked.

I was on my way to Holloway to visit a friend, equipped with spirits and handmade chocolates.

Alcohol made me impulsive and dismissive of stuff I would usually be aware of. I wanted to smoke non-stop despite feeling energised and ready to run a marathon.

I passed a poster on the train platform for a portrait exhibition. Who was this guy? How many portraits did he have to paint in order to merit the title 'portrait artist'? I guess he had to have painted more than one in order to hold a portrait exhibition.

The train had no windows and I was stuck in 12 carriages of sticky English summer, wearing a woollen dress. Jim Morrison whispered in my ears. How the fuck was he so manly at 27 (and before)? I had never met a man with that much testosterone any younger than 32.

"Do you see a future in you two?"

"I see a future of uncertainty and adventure. It is a future, but I have many futures to consider."

A man on the platform picks his nose, rolls the bogey between his fingers for a few seconds then flicks it to the ground. I'm glad my future isn't tied to his. Well, it is. He will exist for most of the time I will also be busy existing. He may even decide how much tax I pay, what coffee beans Starbucks imports, how many cardboard boxes are produced in a factory, he may be unwittingly mapping out my future. All I knew was that his hands were dirty.

I couldn't sit still in the Fens today. I had to head back.

VF was doing a doorstep interview today—more work, great news. I was busy growing agitated by my own existence, but eventually I forced myself out of bed.

I wasn't depressed any more and would not allow it. I would rather be drunk on one glass of red than at home biting my lip. I had choices open to me, and I had to accept whatever choices I had made. Morrissey was singing now.

'Why do you come hereeeee when you know it makes things hard for me?'

I tried to turn him down, which took a few moments of experimentation after realising his voice was coming from my phone and not my laptop.

'I'm soooooo sorry!'

Moscow to Petushki whilst Ladbroke Grove to Baker Street

Plath only wrote one novel. Imagine creating just a single work your whole career. This appeared to be the story behind Venedikt Erofeev, my new found love, courtesy of VF's bookshelf. It held an inscription signed '*Love, L*'. I didn't care to investigate but in the end I couldn't resist.

"So where did you discover this guy?"

"It was a present from a Russian girl I was seeing last year. Haven't read it."

I wondered what the intention was behind the gift. Perhaps she was hoping he would cherish it and become obsessed. The book would serve as a constant reminder of her, even when they no longer spoke. I know I had gifted with the same intention. Little did she know, his girlfriend was getting more joy out of it than he ever did. I doubt he'd notice if it permanently disappeared from his shelf and found its way onto mine. Our shelves would probably be united someday, anyway. I'll keep it.

I loved the idea of writing this huge poetic concept lasting 50 pages. I could easily do the same myself. I should play more with the short story and poem. The poem. The.

'In Petushki the jasmine never stops blooming
and the birds always sing.'

The train swayed from left to right, mostly tilting to the left, and my eyes were gazing to the right. A man around ten years older than me sat opposite. He had a soft, warm, glowing complexion. I wouldn't like to sleep with him, but rather fall asleep in his lap whilst he cradled my cheek with his palm. I pondered talking to him, but his eyes did not stray from the window. Regulars on the train seldom looked out the window, so I reached the conclusion he must be visiting. It wasn't important, I should mind my own business. Maybe if I wasn't so preoccupied with men I'd be writing more, but I enjoyed writing about men more than most things.

I hadn't always had an obsession with men or company, and I wouldn't call it an obsession now. I just found immense comfort in the security men offer, and also an intellect that was more subject than gossip-based, which didn't occur so naturally in my female relationships.

I distracted myself on the train by checking in with my mother over the phone. We spoke for 20 minutes and we arranged to join forces in the hunt for the Cannes dress.

Grey

The day offered little thus far. Grey, unassuming, 09:00. No more lazy bed days for a while. There was no sunshine, no wind, no rain (no pain). It was ok to live quietly and unassumingly for a couple of days.

Upon my arrival back in Fenland the weather took a damp turn. I retired to bed, depressed and numb. I wasn't cut out for stuff like Cannes. I barely made it to my friends' parties, let alone parties in the South of France where I knew nobody. I wasn't suited to the life I was pretending I would be able to live. If I had a reputation as a writer or somebody, anybody at all, then maybe I'd have the confidence to show up somewhere in a dress. Until then, I'd stay at home in bed ignoring my phone and pretending I didn't exist to the outside world.

I apologise for the lack of content today. If I can't express how I'm feeling to myself, then you can only imagine how bad it really feels.

Flat ironing board chest little boy bad haircut tattooed mess misfit unfit nobody in an ill-fitting dress.

<u>Fugitive billionaires</u>

Today we found ourselves outside an apartment block in Oxford Street, London. The apartments housed London's richest and most successful. The people I saw leaving the apartment block didn't look much happier than the people emerging from the tube station opposite. The going rate for an apartment here is £17,000 a month. I would look sour-faced at that price too.

Today we were waiting for a fugitive billionaire who had an arrest warrant against him. I felt I had a punishment set against me, waiting outside his apartment building from 06:00-16:00. 16:00 was when overtime began, so we were sent home at 16:00 by the news people.

VF practised his piece to camera. He rehearsed certain words over. Plain words, the highlights. His words of emphasis always stuck with me. Today that word appeared to be:

'BESOTTED'

He was in no way besotted with the fugitive billionaire but instead I was the source of imagination that led him to use words such as 'besotted'.

We took it in turns to perform coffee runs, toilet breaks and nicotine top-ups. We were on our fourth pack of Richmond Menthol Superkings. I used to smoke better tobacco but I didn't really smoke too much nowadays. Days like today just required a distraction.

We decided our earnings from today would go towards a trip to Morocco. There was no particular reason for Morocco other than the cheap package deals we had seen in the newspaper, and that seemed reason enough to make a trip. We would hire a motorbike and explore the mountains, read next to clear blue pools and drink cocktails.

We made small talk until we ran out. A journalist from a rival station turned up just to say she had been there and cash the cheque. I was introduced as the girlfriend and we continued to stand outside.

Despite the thousands of visitors passing through Oxford Street we had attracted the attention of security. We were questioned about our intentions and purpose. We told them. We continued to wait and kept the small talk going. I popped out to the shops on Oxford Street to buy a pair of trousers and a book for our holiday.

"I bought this book. I need a distraction from reading Proust."

"That is what bothers me—you have such a depth and wealth of knowledge, yet you read shit like that when you should be reading Proust. You talk about stuff I don't want to know, like what you had for breakfast, lunch, dinner. I don't want to know that shit."

"I can read Proust and do other things. It's a balance baby. You need some shit to highlight what you're actually meant to be doing."

"My father used to go to watch rugby games, down in Plymouth where he was born. And my mother would always accompany him, sitting silently by his side, reading Proust. I always imagined I'd be utterly besotted to find a girl who I might walk in on, sitting on the toilet, reading Proust. And here you are. Everything I dreamed of—a girl sat on the toilet reading Proust."

We packed up for the day. No billionaire fugitives were found today, yet still I had managed to besot a man just by sitting on the loo.

We decided our night of freedom after hunting fugitives required a stroll through London. We headed for Waterloo. We walked most places when we could. We passed a mural sprayed on the wall:

'A BAD DAY IN LONDON

IS BETTER

THAN A GOOD DAY

ANYWHERE ELSE'

The wind and rain picked up just as we crossed the Thames. No matter which direction we faced, grey beauty smiled back at us. Perhaps not a smile, but a feeling of reassurance—our London, untouched by anything but the weather.

My scarf struggled to stay around my neck as the wind shook us. Everyone else had finished work too, but walked alone. The path was narrow, so two people holding hands seemed to take up space. We continued to hold hands and walk. A two minute walk took close to ten minutes during a storm. We paused on Waterloo Bridge and VF watched the water flowing underneath.

You seldom see a man clutching your palm and crying on Waterloo Bridge.

I decided I would always be besotted by him too.

Mothers

No other thoughts or words come to mind when I look at the 20 next to March on my calendar.

Happy birthday, Mum.

I wonder what must enter your mind on your birthday. A flashback to your 27th birthday, feeling heavy with the burden of a baby in your womb. Your 40th birthday in the middle of a divorce. Your 20th birthday, still illegal to drink in the foreign country you called home. Your 30th birthday, a toddler monopolising your time.

Mum. Mom.

I hope your 50th birthday is free from pain, children, ex husbands and restriction. Happy 50th, Mom.

I hope you've found a hair colour that suits you after 30 years of experimentation. I hope you're happy with the habits you've taken up and the ones you chose to ditch. The businesses you began and the ones you were forced to end. I hope age brings you peace and a sense of calm. I only hope this is what age bequeathes upon us.

Happy birthday.

Slice a lemon for my drink

I dreamt I was being followed by a Humbert Humbert character. He followed me until I fell for him. A Nabokov and Fowles cocktail shakes my unconscious.

For the first time in weeks (if not months) I had slept deeply through the night. It had begun—the depression was over and my warm glowing friend had returned to comfort me. It was time to change the bed sheets for clean linen, wear tighter clothes and start filling up the diary. I sat down to check my diary for the next two weeks. One play, one party, nothing, and nothing. My pages were so empty I even wrote what colour laundry I would do each day in little green pen.

During the depression I had somehow saved some money in the bank. I was too depressed to go shopping or to restaurants. I started to get big ideas about what to do with this modest sum. Morocco. Just like VF said. And yes, I would sit on the back of a motorbike.

Never had I ventured outside of Europe (with the exception of America) and I was ready to blossom. I was ready to replace my fan fiction books with Proust, I was ready to talk to people again about literature, film and theory. No longer would I find myself worrying what to say at a party—I was writing again.

"Do me a favour will you? Keep away from the windows. Somebody might blow you a kiss. See? It's all about the plosives, baby."

"Slice me a lemon for my cup of corner shop piss vodka. How's that for plosives?"

"Who said that?"

"Me."

"I forgot you're a fucking genius."

We drink into the night doing whatever it is that makes nights fly. I always ensure we have lemons in the fridge.

Electric Ballroom

Depressed Jasmine didn't do spontaneity, but since it had all changed I decided last-minute we would attend a gig at the Electric Ballroom. We pushed our way to the front, snogged each other's mouths covered in sweat, danced and drank to an indie band called Sports Team. As we exchanged goodbyes outside Camden tube station he said:

"I like you even more now, us doing stuff like this. I could never date a girl that stood at the back."

I hopped on the last train home, Fenland bound, to reflect on the words we shared.

"You only write monologues because you don't have other substance to use as a basis."

"Well yeah, it's authentic, it always works on paper."

"Maybe you should put yourself in more scenarios, to talk."

Maybe I should, I thought.

For me, the highlight of conversation is planning the conversations—the words and turns of phrase you want to use, their reactions, the things they won't be thinking, the things they're not expressing. I've becoming quite intuitive when it comes to predicting people's mindsets in a conversation. I don't even know my own habits in terms of the spoken word, but I can dart across different tones, and when nervous my mother's American accent comes out.

I've gotten this train back and forth so many times in my adult life. I know every single turn of the train between London and Fenland.

Tomorrow he will be experiencing the twists and turns of this very train en route to Fenland for my mother's birthday party. Tomorrow more spontaneity and conversation lie ahead. More dialogue. More diary content for you. Nothing more to say for today.

Pinter

I finally stumbled out of the three day haze of alcohol, sickness and insomnia.

I sat in a steaming hot bath dunking bread into chicken soup. My throat was so raw I had given up talking for the rest of the day. The combination of live music plus family and friends wanting to hear every new element of my life had drained me, so I had drained the bottle.

VF and I slept on and off and darted from place to place until our day of rest when I emerged from bed at 17:00 to get ready for the play. Tonight, Pinter.

We walk down towards Holland Park station to make our way to Soho.

"Isn't it fascinating that we walk down here and the buildings are painted in jaunty colours and rosy cheeked little boys on high-vitamin diets surround us, when just a year ago we were on Goldhawk Road. I'm not saying that people are happier here than there, but you can see an obvious difference."

"Living here is making you say words like 'jaunty'."

"Yeah, 'jaunty' is a word you use when you're not poverty-stricken. You know you can tell a lot about an area by the length of the cigarette butts in the gutter."

I take my seat in the Harold Pinter theatre and wait for the curtain to part. A wave of sickness comes over me. I sell my ticket on the door for £40 and run for the next tube home to bed. VF said the play was good, one of Pinter's best. I think it was *The Birthday Party* and maybe one other.

Fenland banger racing

The manic had struck again. I had been pulling all-night benders trying to develop a film concept—one that existed purely in my mind but not yet in that of my audience.

Fen girls who banger race.
The Fen racetrack.
Flatland racers.
Scrap metal.

A lengthy application to the BFI was underway. To justify the importance, the reason, the need to make a film seemed unjust when it existed so purely in my own head. I didn't so much care if there was an audience for it, I just yearned to make it for myself, for selfish reasons.

For years I had battled to make something from the Fens, but the reasoning and medium were not quite there. Yet now I had the perfect subject.

Pre-teen girls living in poverty-stricken, art-devoid, field-upon-field flatlands. I needed to document these girls, be it out of my own pocket or with funding.

I sat in a cushty corner of Notting Hill drinking coffee with rose water (yes really) as I scrawled word after word about my film concept.

VF walked down and we met for a stroll through Holland Park. He was practising his interview techniques for a big job tomorrow. I had to play the part of a CEO who had recently found themselves in the shit. I tried to use all the buzz words I imagined a CEO would use. By the end of the walk I had taken on the hypothetical stress from the situation the CEO's company had found itself in, and the two hours of interviews I had endured. I shook it off and returned to being Jasmine.

I wondered if people in the park overheard the conversations and really believed I was a high-powered Oxford-educated CEO. They probably thought we were practising film lines. I didn't talk too much about the economics of the company, but went for the sympathy vote.

We took a right and headed down towards Shepherd's Bush. VF needed a manicure to ensure he was smart for tomorrow's big gig. I sat and waited, watching him amongst the woman filing nails. I can't afford to get my nails done. I wish VF had offered. We continued down Goldhawk Road and bought fried chicken for dinner. VF wrapped each piece in a paper napkin before passing it to me as we walked through the market, our arms entwined.

I told myself I would never let myself be anything other than a creative. I deserve to earn a living from gathering my thoughts in the sunshine in Holland Park.

Tick this box

Our diet wasn't great. It consisted mainly of eggs, salami, bagels and raw vegetables. Food was a matter of time and convenience. We often ate fried chicken on the go because it was cheap and filling. We rarely ate out because VF found the experience of being waited on uncomfortable. I agree with that. I never let a server pour a drink, I just ask them to leave the bottle and I top myself up—not that I've ordered a bottle of wine in a restaurant more than a handful of times.

We sat in the kitchen, surrounded by drying laundry hanging off every surface. The Moka begins to boil.

"I like coffee, yeah, but I never imagined someone like you to only drink from a Moka. You don't care about food and drink."

"Well, you get vast quantities out of a Moka that you can reheat during the day, so that's one reason. My mother used to make the coffee in a Moka. So I guess it stuck."

VF always put the Moka on the biggest ring and turned the heat up all the way. The coffee was so burnt it was undrinkable. Every bloody day. I chose to drink the burnt coffee rather than make it myself. VF insisted the coffee was fine.

Our backgrounds were similar in the way we spoke about feelings of being a foreign child, stuck in a class we didn't identify with. We both had mothers who had found themselves in foreign countries, relying on men to guide them and be breadwinners.

I don't belong to a class. I wasn't educated. I was entitled to lots of state benefits, being from from a low income background with a single mother. As I grew up I found this once-forgotten background creeping up on me.

'TICK THIS BOX IF YOU WERE ENTITLED TO FREE SCHOOL MEALS'

Filling in data about my background and education bored me deeply. I had spent the last five years remaking myself. I didn't want to have to rely on my past life to create the image of who I am now. I threw the funding applications in the bin. I don't want to belong to any club.

"I'm just talking neurology. If a young child's neural pathways are seared in a certain direction then that's the way the chemistry is structured. Sorry."

I decided I would wire my own brain and that was that. I had the power to choose my own influences nowadays.

Paris

Idleness had gotten to me. I spent day upon day holed up in VF's flat. I tried to garden some days but just couldn't shake off the darkness. Often I would pop Codeine or Tramadol to smooth out the day.

He had put me in touch with a film producer from Cannes, who was interested in some scripts of mine—the diaries. We met for coffee and he seemed interested, then disappeared, never to be seen again.

I couldn't stand London or the Fens.

Nobody wanted me. Nowhere in the world was I wanted.

I knew I couldn't be happy anywhere but it was worth a go.

I took a bus to Paris that lasted eight hours and cost £12. I stayed for two weeks, before returning to the Fens to collect the rest of my belongings and return to Paris.

VF was happy for me. He said Paris would make me. After all, he was the person who first introduced me.

My parents were not bothered and I wasn't particularly close with anyone else, so I barely announced the move.

I found a cosy flat with wooden flooring in the 9th arrondissement. Rue Bergère (meaning female shepherd). It had French windows. That was all I craved.

I had no money for luxuries. There wasn't even a pillow so I slept on a balled-up shirt. The house was empty but Paris was mine.

Summer heatwave

Paris is unbearably hot. I can't walk too far during the day for the heat. My legs are roasting. The day I returned with my suitcase it hit 42 degrees. I didn't have money for a cab or the train so I walked two hours in the heat.

When I got home I sat with my feet in a bowl of cold water. My legs were dirty from the wheels of the suitcase bashing against them.

The flat is close to everything. The neighbours laugh often and I see them eating together.

My English friend JM lives just the other side of the river, so we often drink together. He introduced me to an American friend of his so I have started joining her for walks around town.

I permitted myself a pastry each day, an evening meal and a small glass of wine (always at home). No way can I afford restaurants, apart from the occasional lemonade or coffee with friends.

It has really set in that I will be lonely wherever I am.

I moved to the only place where I thought I would be comfortable, yet I cannot sleep or even leave the house.

I try to walk to the Palais Royal to sit by the fountain every day. Most days I just can't get out of bed.

<u>Bridge alert</u>

I still had no inspiration to read or write. I would sit by the fountains and in the parks, but felt useless. I have nothing to write about, no friends and no true lovers left anymore.

VF wrote most days but often in the form of long emails in the early hours. The emails scared me. Some days he loved me and some days not.

Many nights I fantasised about jumping off the Pont Neuf or Pont des Arts into the Seine. That would be that.

I had to avoid bridges for a while.

This isn't a raging angry sadness, it is a peaceful sadness.

My parents and two friends came to visit for my birthday. Still, no light. It made me feel even worse. It made me feel like I could not appreciate anything and should be punished.

In the early hours of the morning I sat on a bench atop the Pont des Arts, gently crying and wishing for anything but sadness.

Pastis

A few days after my birthday VF came to visit. I picked him up in the afternoon from Gare du Nord and walked him down to my flat. He was wearing a light grey suit. It seemed odd. I think he had convinced himself he was James Bond on assignment.

VF made me feel a little better. We drank sickly sweet cheap white wine on the island (this was after the Notre Dame fire) and watched the boats sail by. I liked to wave to the children.

VF went to meet his godawful friend on the left bank and I met him later that evening at Les Deux Magots. I had always wanted to dine there but it was too expensive so we had Pastis and olives (I don't like olives, so he ate those).

It was clear by this point Paris had nothing more to offer me than beauty. I spoke to VF about my overwhelming sadness and he suggested I get a job.

I had always told myself if I reached the end of the line emotionally I would join the army or become a nurse. That way at least I could be useful to society.

The next day I applied for a job as a nurse.

Diabetes nursing

I put the Moka on to boil and made small talk with the cleaner. She was a new lady I hadn't seen before. She had huge round eyes, the kind sort. She looked warm and neat, though lanky. She moved fast and did an excellent job.

I offered her a cup of coffee. She said the coffee smelt fancy. I told her it was Aldi coffee beans. On my working days I just drank instant.

I downed two cups and slunk into town in a summer dress. 28 degrees. I was excited by these hot summers but the days never matched up to my initial excitement. I bought an iced coffee for the hell of it and a newspaper. I sat in two different parks in Cambridge whilst I read my paper and smoked.

My hospital apartment was a 40 minutes' walk from town. I worked three days or nights per week, so I had a lot of time on my hands, studying aside. I liked working the night shifts on the wards so I could study. The nights were far quieter.

Nobody wanted to spend time with me today, or at least that's how it felt. I watched people pass. Perhaps they chose to sit on this side of the green to be near me, but nobody spoke. I am not the main character.

I grew tired of my own company so retreated home to my hospital digs. Nobody called me and I didn't care to call anyone. I read it was Kate Bush's birthday in the paper. I listened to *The Dreaming* and slumped back into my depression on linen sheets.

I am working on the diabetes ward tomorrow. The staff bore me. Diabetes is quite a boring disease.

Cold pasta

I held their hands.

A 16-year-old girl was trying to extinguish herself whilst I sweated to save the lives of people four times her age. Another day.

I knew how the young girl felt. The mental health patients made me feel uncomfortable.

I ate a bowl of cold pasta and scrolled my phone, avoiding conversation with my colleagues. One nurse was obsessive about my writing. I didn't want to talk to him. I told a few people I had come from Paris for the job. Mostly I didn't speak.

I mostly changed dressings and helped on the medication rounds. Today we had a few amputations.

Sorry, I don't like to write about nursing. I've been nursing for eight months now and I can't think of anything to put down.

My birthday is approaching and I intentionally have no plans.

I deserve to wallow at home alone. I don't care.

A week in bed

I was on day five in bed. I hadn't told anybody because I feared the consequences. Being dragged out to sit in silence opposite someone in a cafe. Even worse, being dragged to a doctor. It was fine for now. If I didn't overcome it by next week I guess there would be trouble.

Only three days at work next week. Three days of nursing the obese, the sick, the elderly and the delirious. I couldn't stand the thought. I didn't deserve this but it also served as punishment for my depression.

My atonement.

Filthy work for an ungrateful young woman.

Next week would be the decider. I had to go to work or I had to quit.

Quit nursing and start writing again.

Where would I live? Would I grow more depressed? I can't imagine being more depressed than I am now.

Last week was my birthday. I took codeine, floated around Portobello Road and napped the rest of the day.

Last Thursday VF took me to Berlin.

I spent those five days in bed. I am an ungrateful fuck.

European summer holidays, new cities. I spent the entire time depression-sleeping with the exception of one coffee shop and one bar. Pathetic. I never liked Berlin. It lacked identity. It was just a mess of different identities. But we did eat and drink well. Plus, one night I actually visited the film director I hadn't seen in many years. He was still annoying.

The minute I walked through my Cambridge apartment door I threw the suitcase atop my wardrobe and crawled into bed for the rest of the day.

VF had gone onto Italy after Berlin while I returned to the UK. I couldn't face time with other people. A fucking burden. I certainly couldn't go to Italy.

The highlight of my holiday was sketching the floor tiles of the rented apartment whilst VF watched football at a bar round the corner.

I'll say it again, pathetic.

I had slept from 09:00-15:00 after a full night's sleep. I showered then walked to the grocery store half a mile from the hospital. I bought sanitary pads, chocolate and precooked chicken. I returned to bed for the remainder of the night. Nobody rang today. Nothing else to report.

I thought my writing would be better than this by now.

Pathetic

I awoke mid-morning with a new idea. I was allowed to leave the house. I had a couple of thousand pounds. I could go anywhere I pleased—a steam train to Dungeness, a flight to Eastern Europe. Yet here I was, destined to remain in bed. I suppose this proves I would never have been happy in Paris, even if I could afford to go out to restaurants.

VF called it 'measles of the brain' and begs me to stay positive. Instead I excuse myself and allow depression to drift over me like a wet cloud.

"Let's banish this word 'pathetic'. You use it on yourself and on me. It's an awful, compassionless sentiment that says more about the user than the object. Its true meaning is 'to arouse sympathy', not its bastardised form. Neither you, nor anybody else, is worthy of that contempt."

I am allowed to be pathetic.

I shower and dress then sit at my desk and dream of my bed. I had not eaten a hot meal since Saturday night in Berlin. I would try to cook something today. There was a fridge of healthy food rotting away as I lay in bed. Another job I guess. Restock the fridge. Throw the contents of the fridge in the bin. Rinse and repeat.

I took a couple of beta blockers to permit an odyssey to the kitchen to try to make breakfast.

<u>Nurses who spend the day in bed</u>

I examined my face in the mirror. Just past midnight, probably. This could have been at any stage of my life. Pre-puberty in my childhood home, the morning after a one night stand, or predictably, alone in my bedroom. My face was always the same. I can't remember it ever being different.

The depression had lifted to the point that I could leave the house once a week, but I still didn't feel the urge to do anything. I did escape the bed before noon the last two days and told myself I would go work at the hospital.

Why are you a nurse?

My fucking atonement.

Stop it. I had started to enjoy my sick punishment, but after Covid and the elderly it felt wretched. Maybe that had refuelled my depression? The misery. The sickness. Days on end staring at the walls. I, their nurse, their sole source of conversation and entertainment. Little Jasmine did not have the bandwidth for war stories and tales of old England, dashing between 12 dying men.

I didn't think of work when I was at home, apart from the children who had died. I thought of them often.

I had no thoughts of men, friends or family recently. I lived inside my own empty bubble. As if doped up on antidepressants, I felt numb to all. I listened to the radio, rewrote poems and sorted my postage stamps.

Not a single thought crossed my mind. Two months had passed without reflection. Berlin. Cambridge. London. Different cities to sleep and shit in. I hate to say it. I couldn't appreciate anywhere unless it had a bed and toilet nearby. I am too much a creature of comfort.

The days of wanting to travel the world—book tours, lovers. They were gone. I was destined for a life in a coffin-shaped room working 20:00-08:00 on the wards. The world slept whilst I nursed.

I had become accustomed to sleeping during the daytime. In fact I enjoyed it. I could exist alone, in peace.

VF seldom writes but is glad I am nursing.

Until tomorrow.

<u>The scale</u>

I woke up more depressed today than when I left the world yesterday. How is that even possible? I guess knowing there is a whole day yawning ahead does that. I will try to shower and make breakfast before I start to write. I need to write again. I need an existence outside hospital life, even within my own head.

If I was so depressed, why couldn't I just funnel my focus into writing as a punishment? I guess I lacked the attention span. I just didn't care.

I checked my bank account to ensure 30% of my wage had gone out on rent, leaving enough money to see me through the next 25 days sitting at home.

Yes, perfect. I could save a lot of money too. Nursing paid better than any job that I had worked before—though that bar was pretty low. If I was frugal I could save £600 a month. I bought nothing anyway, apart from food.

I decided I would crawl out of bed before noon and make eggs and iced coffee for breakfast. Maybe it would give me the energy to work. I felt no desire to stay in bed, I felt the desire to 'do'. My depression had tipped from an eight back down to a six.

VF had requested I tell him where I stood on my depression scale each day. I would wake up and automatically write six.

Six was depressed but manageable.
Eight was curtains drawn, phone off, duvet all day.

Six was just able to go into work. I would float at a six today, with peaks of a five whilst working then a seven before bed.

The worst part about waking up was knowing nobody in the world desired you, craved you. You awoke alone with no future plans. Not a single person you passed in the street, spoke to at a party, who read your book, not a single person wanted to spend the day with you. The day was your own and you filled the lonely void with your own entertainment. That is why most days started with a six.

I poached eggs and continued to sit in the void. As I existed alone, no thoughts passed until I started to write them down. I need some human interaction.

It reminded me of the first time I took antidepressants aged 16. I sat on a train from King's Lynn to Ely, a half hour journey. During that time not a single thought went through my mind. Asleep with my eyes open. Just floating. If I didn't move, speak or write, nothing existed.

I slept the remainder of the day and reemerged from my slumber at 20:00 to make dinner and smoke a cigarette. It was hospital accommodation so we had to smoke outside. None of the other nurses here smoked.

I fiddled with my camera to replace the film with a new roll. I had a bought my first ever camera with my nurse's wages. It was from the 1970s and Japanese. I had only developed one roll of film so far which hadn't turned out very well. I was still practising.

I remembered moving to a new town for the first time. Every act was romantic. Exploring the city at night, the first drink in a bar, dates with older men—that excitement. Now the rush felt so unattainable, so distant. Another girl in another life. I considered taking a walk tonight with my camera, but knew it wasn't worth it. I wouldn't be home until 23:00 even if I left now. I loved Cambridge streets at night, but it took a lot to motivate me to leave the house for anything but work.

When I was younger and lonely I would spend all my time out. I would stroll the streets hoping to meet someone, anyone. I seldom did because Fen folk are mostly elderly. Yet I would walk and sit on benches waiting for something, anything. Each night I would leave home just to walk around and sit on a bench under a street lamp.

I like that idea, upon reflection. Maybe I could do that Thursday.

I lay in bed close to midnight daydreaming of the warmer climates I would one day travel to. Villages of golden maize, terracotta houses and lightly-spiced delicacies. Another time, when I am better.

Flip

Again life had flipped. The axis tilted. The switch. I was happy again. Three out of ten on the scale.

I had spent the day dashing around—studying, writing, pampering myself, socialising.

Even fucking. Yes, fucking.

I was swimming in a pool of lovey slush. A junior doctor my age. The excitement of it all. I had forgotten how exciting new romances could be. At work I daydreamed of him whilst nursing, of what experiences we would share that evening. He lived ten minutes up the road, practically the same street. Every night I spent at his house. The sex was amazing. Depression had drained me of inspiration, even desire, for years.

Did I just need to get laid to get it back? Whatever 'it' is. The passion for life.

Apparently so.

Nah. It's mental illness.

Who the fuck knows. I'm happier because I got laid by a sexy junior doctor.

I look forward to work in the morning.

<u>The day after the night before</u>

Again I was depressed. I lay in bed the entirety of the day.

The doctor told me to stop saying 'thank you' each time we had sex. He had introduced me to his friends. He even drove us to the beach one day. We did a lot of ketamine and coke. He took antidepressants too. I saw them on his desk. But depressed boys couldn't save me.

Hello depression.

Now I didn't crave anything.

<u>More about that doctor</u>

The Sertraline kept me going through the days as I plodded along between smoking, napping and drinking. I mostly cross-stitched pictures or words during the day, and commuted between mine and his.

I had decided relationships were overrated and I would rather work towards my writing. Pens don't get mood swings. I would always prefer my own peace and quiet. Time to lay low for a few days.

Work was depressing and a burden. I might once have seen nursing in a holy light, but now it feels a cruel necessity. If someone was forced to look after me in my dotage I would simply end it myself. The embarrassment of being dependent on anyone for anything.

10:00. I sit in bed alone and write throughout the day, no need to leave.

"Thank you for inviting me over."

"I'm not doing you a favour. Stop saying 'thank you'."

I argued it was in my nature to be courteous and wanted him to see my appreciation. But he was on coke and maybe just wanted to prove a point. There was no power struggle but this pissed me off. Undermining my personality for being too polite. Fuck off.

My writing felt damaged by all the lust and excitement, so I decided to let the desire fade away.

If he asked to see me again it would be my rules—he could meet me for drinks or take me out. I didn't want to exist in his parallel universe anymore. We only ever met at his house. It is a red flag when you only ever meet a boy at his house.

Too much give. Time to play it cool. I could have any man I wanted.

I'm not manic, just purely observational.

My feelings remained strong though dulled by the Sertraline. It suited me fine.

I slept all day like a child with chronic illness. I awoke and felt even less motivation. I hadn't eaten in 24 hours and this barely concerned me. My body felt numb too. I could barely write without taking a break to stare at the wall every other sentence.

Even music sounds wrong right now. You know when you're in a depression warp when voices sound different and time moves at a different pace. That is where I'm at.

I am trying to perceive each day as a window rather than a fully built house. Every day I can work on the window, build a little of the frame, varnish it, perhaps even smile at my reflection. I cannot build a house in one day and it is pointless to hope I can, no matter how manic. Houses, relationships, whatever.

<u>Binning the flowers</u>

I walked into Cambridge town to drink coffee and sit with the cows. It was warm for September, 17 degrees. I didn't need the double cashmere.

I met two friends.

I could not focus on anything—friendships, career, lover? No.

I had not eaten today and did not care to. Being hungry would, if nothing else, force me to sleep more. Good.

Time moves at a different pace when you are desperate. Since I hit 20 years old time has moved faster anyway.

A bunch of flowers arrived in the mail as a sympathy gift for the passing of Nana Y. She had died in the hospital where I work.

I snapped the twigs in half and binned them. Another thing to care for. I couldn't. I didn't have a vase anyhow.

<u>Day ? in bed</u>

I regretted chucking the flowers. I dusted my bedside table and window, rearranging the dried flowers. Dead flowers suited my lifestyle better.

I was dressed and out of bed at a decent hour for the first time in aeons. My period had begun and I felt a little more human.

Practise escapism with more integrity. Seek knowledge not possessions. I sat and did my reading for the day. Back to the nurse grind. I enjoyed studying medicine and anatomy. It gave me a purpose and I could do it from my bedroom. I could be a nurse from my bedroom. I just hated working on the wards surrounded by death and filth.

VF phoned this morning. He said he and a friend had concluded nurses were up there with combat veterans in PTSD terms, and I shouldn't take it lightly. I agreed.

I spent more time thinking about the death I had witnessed.

Suicide attempts every day.

One man had chainsawed off his own arms.

Nursing wasn't what I thought it would be.

<u>Another day spent in bed</u>

30 days hath September.

I had near enough given up on my pathetic attempt at romance (doing drugs in a junior doctor's bedroom for three weeks) and, near enough, the appeal had disappeared from my mind.

All night the voices laughed at me. I dreamt I was mocked all night. Nothing but continuous laughter. Despite the endless guffawing I had managed to sleep eight hours or so.

My dreams were vivid and always set in Paris, but a watery Venice version.

I had no plans for the day though upon waking I impulsively asked VF to travel up and look after me. VF knows how to care for me. I hoped he would show up by noon and take me out for a walk. I continued to hide under the sheets but wrote whenever a thought crossed my mind. I took my morning dose of Sertraline and rolled back over.

Nothing beats new romance excitement. Nothing comes close. You can romanticise a stranger.

But one day the spirit just dies. It dies a natural death. Lack of water, care. It just dies.

Baths in Notting Hill

I fell out of my depression slowly and gradually. I ate, read, watched TV and took two baths a day. Once a day I would stroll down Portobello Road for a coffee or beer. I was slowly recovering.

All my traumas had intertwined, like multiple tangled pairs of stockings washed and hung up to dry. It felt near impossible to address any issue. The failed romances, my growing hatred of nursing, my lack of close friends. It all stemmed back to my lack of confidence.

I stayed in bed until late morning with VF. We no longer had sex. We just stretched out, limbs entwined, sleeping as much as we could. Anyone would think he was depressed too. He insisted not. I suppose he was just exhausted from looking after me. Nobody could see me in a romantic light when I was like this. I don't blame them.

I didn't want to jump off a bridge anymore. But I couldn't be bothered to leave the house. Which is the bigger issue?

Back to Cambridge

Drunk.

I decided alcohol would be my new vice.
Easier.
Innit.

Not a single man in London, Cambridge or Europe wanted me tonight.

'The sea wants to take me. The night wants to slit me.'

My melancholy is louder than bombs. I sleep until noon and stare at the walls for the rest of the day.

I told the hospital I was too ill to work. My doctor (not the one I was shagging) wrote me a sick note for two months.

I didn't have to look after sick people anymore.

Back to Notting Hill

I fled to London on the first train I could.

The melancholy was stronger than ever. I'd drawn up my will years ago.

I mostly slept during the day, there was nothing else to do. I was not working or socialising. I simply drowsed and dreaded waking up. What a waste of time and resources, if nothing else.

I didn't crave dying, just that sweet release of sleep one desires after a long day. To those who abjure suicide—do you not long for a peaceful night's sleep after a hard day at work? I have been hard at work my whole life and it seems I don't get paid. There is no reward for long days.

Suicide took motivation though, which I had none of. It used to be far easier to kill yourself. Head in the oven. VF said our oven wouldn't work. In 2020 you had to get creative. I had access to all kinds of drugs at work. But that seemed too artificial, synthetic. I would like to die a good old fashioned way. But trains and leaps from tall buildings hurt. Perhaps drowning was the best alternative. Rocks in pockets. I don't know. Again, too much effort.

I sat on the Victoria line from Tottenham Hale to King's Cross. I hoped I would turn up to find a girl on his sofa. A small, helpless girl. A girl who thought herself romantic and edgy but felt belittled at the sight of me. I was the only girl he could ever value at an intellectual level equal to his own. He had told me he was dating. Surely he couldn't find an equivalent on Tinder in one week.

He said she was from up north. She had gotten the train down. At least she would have a terrible accent.

139

I downed two vodka cranberries on the train to soothe my nerves, ready to annihilate whichever girl I found on his sofa.

Fuck. Why didn't I just turn up unannounced? Rookie error. I could have had more fun that way.

Maybe I wanted to fight for an hour, then I could relax. I guess that was it. I didn't really want to cause harm—I just wanted love.

That's the thing, which game do I play? Am I unconditionally kind, or mean? Sweet or intimidating? I do not know which way to turn. It is always a struggle. I barely know myself, who I am. How could I decide in front of an audience?

I couldn't imagine a busy life ever again. Men came and went faster than I changed my opinion. I was stuck in my own idle line of life.

No girl on the sofa

I arrived a couple hours too late. There was no girl on the sofa. The bins were emptied. The sheets were changed.

We drank vodka and juice in the garden and again on Portobello Road. The pubs closed early due to Covid, so we relied on corner shop vodka for the rest of the night.

VF admitted we were soulmates, but that the relationship didn't work.

I awoke with my head in the toilet. VF was sitting on the bath edge smoking and waiting for me to sober up. He slept on the sofa and I in the bed.

I knew it was reckless but I didn't regret coming. I enjoyed our frivolous evenings, just as long as we didn't fall in love all over again.

West London to East London

The world is so big and magical. Then you go home to your bed and suddenly it seems small again.

I spent three days in London snorting cocaine, watching Italian cinema and French kissing a 60-year-old film director. I really outdid myself this time, right?

The world seemed shrunken but manageable. I no longer craved sleep all day. I know I've written this before, but did I just need to get laid? Is it as simple as that? I was busy. So busy. Ideas. Writing. Looking after myself.

I hadn't spoken to him since leaving his house in Shoreditch. He lived in Andalusia but also owned a place here (a native Londoner).

I could not tell you where the attraction lay but I guess it was mutual understanding and his inquisitive nature. He wanted to hear every story and I was more than happy to share. To new beginnings. Thank you, PW.

<u>Said new beginning</u>

Following days of bedridden depression I had yet to return to the hospital. I tried one day. I seldom write about the hospital, but let me tell you.

A plastic surgery unit. Burns victims. Failed suicide attempts. Hit and run car accidents. What kind of place is this for a girl like me? I thought nursing would bring me a sense of perspective, but instead I felt devastated by humanity and our need to hurt each other or ourselves.

I received my handover from the nightshift nurse with tears streaming down my face. I could not stop crying. I wore glasses at work and we had to wear face masks. I was glad, for my entire face was wet and red.

They told me I wasn't well enough to work, so I headed home to sleep for the day.

I still had no desire to return to work. My depression had lifted, I had money, I had returned to Cambridge, but my love of nursing had vanished.

My mind explored the possibility of a new life. Andalusia with PW. I would take early morning walks across the Spanish countryside whilst I pondered my writing. PW would do the same, drinking coffee whilst reading scripts. We would both work quietly in our Spanish home before reuniting in the late afternoons for lovemaking and home-cooked meals.

I had spent two nights in his company. I had to discard this fantasy.

But the fantasy was motivation to leave bed before noon for the first time in months, so there were benefits.

I had slept peacefully. Half a day back in Cambridge and I was getting back into a good routine. I awoke at 07:00, made scrambled eggs then walked down to one of the university libraries to do my writing.

When I returned home I would do my laundry, make a light lunch then take coffee in Norfolk with a friend.

How long can this daydream of Andalusia fuel me? Place your bets now.

The coffee was cold and my mind was preoccupied. I couldn't wait to escape Norfolk. One drink and off I ran.

I value my friends. I adore my friends. But nothing compares to romance. Romance is a fuck whilst friendship is a smile in the street.

I told myself to be patient and wait until tomorrow before I ran back to the film director.

I took a beer by Cambridge train station on the way home with my girlfriend FN. We went back to hers to eat takeout and watch Daria. I read her some of my recent diaries and we watched YouTube interviews with the new man. FN was always a good one. Not reliable, but always solid when needed. She said she enjoyed the new diaries but was surprised at the darkness of them.

I slept well.

<u>Second date</u>

"Do you want to see me again?"

"Jasmine. First, yes very much. Second. if I didn't it would be very clear, so don't worry. I am overburdened with empathy which is just as bad as not having enough in my opinion."

"Don't do it out of empathy."

"The one good thing about having some years behind you is as much as possible I only do what I want. Don't fret. Looking forward to it."

I awoke practically kicking and jumping. I would take a train to Shoreditch later that day for our second date.

I spent the morning reading the history behind the name 'Shoreditch'. I wanted to learn about my new home. There was no clear answer, but apparently Shakespeare used to hang out there.

Anyway, I would take coffee with FN again, buy groceries and maybe write a little before I hopped on a train. I donned brown cashmere trousers and a black cashmere jumper with a matching scarf.

Last time PW had asked me:

"What message are you trying create through the clothes you choose to wear?"

I told him I just like to be comfortable in lots of layers, and simplistic. I loved my cashmere. Time to leave.

I wrote to VF today. I told him each time I exited the depression and passed into the manic, I felt like I was levelling up in a video game. Each new reward was greater. I hopped from a 50-year-old journalist to 60-year-old filmmaker. Is that a level up?

VF said he couldn't wait to see the last level.
Christ, what would that be?

I downed a ginger and lemon tea and ran for the train.

Cowboy boots

I haven't written in weeks, and boy if I had, the content would have been amazing. I can only apologise.

PW had a girlfriend. I spent one last night in his company in Shoreditch then departed upon this revelation. I asked if we could make something serious together, and he told me about the girl. I was devastated he had lied. I did not have him down as a liar. If my friends lied I would be angry. I was furious with him.

Of course I fled back to VF. He picked me up from the train.

We stopped off at a cafe on Portobello Road where he bought me breakfast. The waitress asked if I was Jasmine Christi. I said yes. She said she liked my book.

The next few days were grim. I cannot remember the precise sequence of events. I spent a few days on VF's sofa and seldom left the house.

On an unremarkable Sunday, VF went out to play football. He invited his young new female friend to grab a drink afterwards. I was invited too. I didn't like their friendship. I saw how they interacted. His jokes went over her head. Her sole motive seemed to sit and look pretty. I bought her a drink and she did not thank me. I knew they had slept together.

VF played football and I walked around Holland Park, visiting the Kyoto Gardens. I sat and watched the kids with their families, the squirrels and the famous peacocks. The peacocks made me feel calm and think of Saraswati.

I had an idea on the walk home. I would find any drugs I could, down everything I had found, curl up beside the pond at the Kyoto Garden and slowly die overnight in my sleep. I would be found in the morning, wrapped up in my warm cashmere coat but stone cold, surrounded by koi carp and peacocks.

I walked back to VF's house where I found half a bottle of pills that were four years out of date. I downed them with orange juice and walked back to my Japanese garden. An hour passed and not much happened. I felt light-headed but that was all. Another hour passed. I deemed the attempt a failure and walked home.

I awoke in bed a few hours later, covered in vomit with half-digested chalky white pills dribbled down my chin. VF was on the phone, slapping my cheek to wake me. I spent the night in Chelsea and Westminster hospital.

An overweight woman with green hair sat by the bedside watching my every move. I sat and stared at the walls. I was hooked up to an ECG, my blood pressure hectic.

"Am I a red special?"

"Yes. We can talk if you want. If not, we don't have to."

I had to 'special' at work as a nurse. People that were a suicide risk needed 24/7 supervision and were assigned someone to sit at their bedside.

An hour later a psychiatrist arrived. He was wearing brown cowboy boots with silver buckles. I could hear the nurses outside joking about his boots. I couldn't take a psychiatrist in cowboy boots seriously.

He pried and tried to make me confess it was arguing with VF that sparked my stupidity. I tried to explain no such thing had occurred. I was pure numb through and through, I had no energy to fight and argue. He seemed way too dumb to have made it through medical school. He couldn't comprehend that nothing had provoked this.

Every suggestion he made was absurd. I had no respect for him and made it obvious—probably why he discharged me as soon as my heart had settled down. He handed me a leaflet containing a phone number, then returned me to the streets at 03:00. He also doubled my prescription, saying I was on too low a dosage.

I had to wait for a nurse to remove my cannula. I took it out myself and the head nurse stopped by to scold me.

VF was waiting for me out front. He summoned an Uber.

I slept for a day and when I awoke I felt exactly the same. VF was on the couch.

"I don't want to wake up next to a dead girl, imagine how bad that would look." I trust he was joking.

The numbness continued and I decided I would try again. I downed all my antidepressants. VF ran towards me and slapped me hard on the back, forcing me to vomit up the soggy pills.

He said he couldn't do this anymore. He called my parents and begged them to help him.

I was shipped back to the Fens the following morning, to call a box room my home.

The second lockdown

England was now in a second Covid lockdown which my parents took very seriously. I slept most of the days but tried to be creative. I had few possessions with me and could not return home to my Cambridge flat to collect more. I had sewing stuff and a few books.

There was no income any more, so it was best to sit at home and sleep. I was not well enough to work. I could barely socialise without attempting to top myself. My parents found it odd I slept so much, but I had no other option. I think the pills had a lot to do with that too.

One day I took a walk, which I actually quite enjoyed (aside from the mud). Next day I attempted to make a wreath, which kept popping out of shape. Some days I would try to make a collage out of old magazines, but they were also suicide themed. I hid them from my parents in a notebook stored in my handbag.

My appetite had not returned. I ate one meal a day late at night and quit alcohol for the time being. My parents were heavy drinkers, imbibing a couple of bottles of wine per evening. I did not want anything to tamper with my mood.

I had no plans for the future. My money would last three months and that was that. I could not face a job. I handed in my notice at the hospital. My mother proposed I permanently move into their village cottage.

Whilst I tried to keep myself together he spent time with the new female friend. I had cut off all contact with him and felt more isolated than ever.

One idea occurred—I could contact my grandfather in Colorado about going to stay on his ranch for a month or two. England had nothing left for me. A change of scenery might help. I had the money for the plane ticket. It varied between £150-£400 for a single ticket, which seemed reasonable.

I lacked the motivation to contact him. Whilst I was depressed I had not replied to his messages, but I would like to contact him over the next week or so to see if this was a possibility.

I would continue to ignore VF for as long as I could. I had a daydream about sending him a postcard from Colorado in February. I imagined how much that would stump him.

I no longer spoke or thought of PW. He was back in Andalusia with his lover.

I have no lovers for now.

New home

About a month had passed and the suicidal idealisations had mostly disappeared. The idea now felt absurd and foreign. My doctor took me off Sertraline and tried me on something else, which I like for now.

I had left my mother's, packed up my Cambridge flat and moved in with my father in nearby Ely. He had erected a bookshelf for me which I filled with my most meaningful possessions.

1. A framed feather from my father's pet pigeon.
2. A bottle of Halfeti perfume.
3. A toy mouse in a nurse's uniform.
4. A wooden box that I stored my hair clips in.
5. A white porcelain dish with Nana Y's rings.

I would look at the items on my shelf each day and feel thankful I had woken another day to peruse my few beautiful possessions.

On the desk I kept a small digital radio that belonged to Nana Y. Next to the radio was a portable record player with four hours' battery life. I hope I can take it to the beach when the weather warms up.

This morning I had listened to Supertramp because they are upbeat.

*'DON'T YOU LOOK AT MY GIRLFRIEND.
SHE'S THE ONLY ONE I'VE GOT.'*

I had a small glass carafe with a stalk of dried cotton, wheat and dusty pink Astilbe.

My new home.

I had no privacy here, living with my father. He didn't allow me to smoke. But I was being proactive and going out most days. The Covid lockdown was still in place so you could not socialise indoors, but I took walks with friends during the day. Some days we drank beer by the river. It seemed strange that once we were free to behave as we pleased. No longer could I up and go to Paris; not even a one night stand in Cambridge. We were all hostages in our own homes.

Saying that, when the virus levels receded I did manage to travel to Berlin with VF last August. The summer was nearly back to normal—six people could gather indoors together and eat at a restaurant. Even eating out was encouraged, for the sake of the economy.

My mother had grown more distant but I didn't mind. We never spoke about my attempt. I felt more comfortable being on my own and independent, there were fewer worries this way. I really do not like to trouble people.

My love life was non-existent by choice. I had many an offer but without breaking the lockdown rules it was tough. Dates consisted of walks through the Fens and a swift goodbye when the rain became unbearable and your hands were too cold to roll a cigarette.

However, VF did come to visit on one fabulous day.

VF does the Fens

We corresponded only via email at this point. Phones complicated what should be simple—communication. Phones should be no more than a convenience, yet everybody clings to them like safety devices. Technology made me anxious and I avoided it as much as possible. My phone lived in a drawer most days.

We planned to meet in Ely for a walk. I had not seen him since the overdose. I had no strong feelings or expectations for the day, it was simple—a walk.

I chose a day with a clear forecast. My friends often joked I was obsessed with the weather. In Paris, the French would mock me for my weather fixation. I plan my days religiously around clouds, wind, rainfall.

Tuesday appeared clear with sunshine in the afternoon, around five degrees. I set my hair the night before and painted my nails. I wore Nana Y's long black cotton coat with brown leather boots. I met VF at the train station that morning and the weather behaved exactly as predicted.

VF was exactly as I remembered him. He wrapped his face with a burgundy cashmere scarf as we walked along the river. VF was a perfect angel and I tried my hardest to be good. I wanted to prove I had truly changed for the better.

"I have not felt this way since I was perhaps fifteen years old."

It was true. I couldn't remember such peace and tranquility. Nothing in the world could break my mood. The depression had finally lifted. VF could have pulled out his phone and showed me pictures of his new girlfriend and I would have smiled and complimented her hair. The world was suddenly calm and whatever I wanted it to be. Finally.

My new antidepressants were dubbed 'baby ecstasy' online. I was constantly on a high—music sounded good again, people were kind once more. I didn't care if I had to swallow medication to feel good. I only hoped it would not wear off too fast. There seemed few side effects either. I slept less, no headaches, no acne, a little weight gain but I was hoping for that after years of being too lazy to cook.

VF was over the moon at my new existence. It wasn't boisterous or loud. It was peaceful and content. I did not want to shout and scream but simply sit quietly and appreciate life, which I did.

I think I saw VF cry tears of joy that day. He was awestruck by my turnaround. I told him over email but I don't think he believed me. During our muddy walk he said:

"Stop being so nice to me. I could cry. Don't use up all your niceness at once."

"Freud said laughter is the opposite of envy, but you eventually run out. I disagree."

It sounded wanky but I heard it on Radio 4 a few days ago. I can't remember his response but he probably laughed. I was secretly worried the happiness would run dry like the riverbed we sat and watched from the granary up a hill somewhere in Morocco.

Christi does Notting Hill, again

Of course the walk went better than anyone could have predicted. We laughed the entire day as we walked hand in hand around the Fens. The sun soon said goodbye and it was time to part. I ended up on the train home with him.

On the train VF said he missed my cooking and craved my French onion soup for dinner. I bought six brown onions, white wine and Gruyere. At his home I got to work caramelising the onions over the course of two hours.

Back when I was depressed I used to dread his home. Wet towels draped over the kitchen door, a sink full of dishes, muddy football boots. I don't know if it was the medication but I found myself unbothered by all of the things that would have triggered me into an obsessive madness. Or maybe his house was particularly clean this time.

He slept on the sofa whilst I made dinner. I wish I could make him dinner every night. His flat was too small for the two of us, and he did not want to move to the Fens.

He drank two bowls of soup and finished off my bowl too. I felt like a mother bird feeding her catch of worms to a fledgling who ate until he was full then curled into a ball. I could spend my entire life catching worms for him, just to watch him sleep peacefully.

The next couple of days went somewhat the same. I cooked and cleaned, he slept. It was pure bliss.

We walked down to Portobello Road, hand in hand. I bought sweet potatoes, nutmeg, sage and parmesan. I spent the afternoon making gnocchi. It was good to literally get stuck into something. The dough covered my hands up to my wrists. I spent the whole afternoon in the kitchen.

Two years on his insomnia was still an issue. We had changed beds, medication, sleep hygiene, but nothing seemed to work. He was haunted by nightmares of failing exams, breaking his camera and being humiliated by his father. Sometimes he dreamt he was at war. At night he tossed and turned. I couldn't do much but hold him and stroke his hair.

I now slept peacefully and easily. Sleep was no longer an issue.

I coated the sweet potato gnocchi in sage butter, crushed pistachios and parmesan. VF cleaned his plate and mine. He teased:

"Why do you only ever make enough for one meal? Why not make some for tomorrow too?"

I wasn't sure. I think I probably enjoyed the process of cooking more than eating, plus I liked to make new dishes each day and walk down to the market in the mornings. It was an excuse to leave the house, a purpose, something to fight off the ever-threatening depression.

Aside from eating and sleeping I did little else. VF had planned a surprise treat for Thursday. I hoped it was something calm like afternoon tea or a museum. We took the underground to Euston Square where we walked ten minutes to The British Museum. VF blagged tickets using his press pass—he told them I was there on work experience. I thought I might get a press card for myself one day. The young man at the ticket office said:

"I hope I get a good write up!"

There would be no write up.

The exhibition was named Tantra. It displayed Hindu and the occasional Buddhist sculpture dating from 800 AD to the present day. One stone sculpture depicted a man performing cunnilingus on an upside down woman with her head in an uncomfortable position.

"Why haven't we ever tried that?"

We hadn't had sex in a long time, but we could joke.

The items on display seemed mostly of Hindu deity Kali. During Religious Studies at college she had always scared me. Her tongue was always poking out of her mouth and she nearly always carried a severed head while dancing on the dead. I did however discover she was the inspiration for the Rolling Stones logo—that massive tongue poking out.

I talked VF through some of the stories of the different gods and goddesses I recalled from my school days. I was hoping to catch Saraswati but she was not there. I loved her grace.

We left the museum and got a McDonald's on the way home. We sat outside in the early evening air before grabbing the underground back home. VF was still hungry so I made an avocado and tomato salad. We had hit the avocado jackpot—20p each on Portobello Road. VF bought 20, so I had to incorporate avocado into every meal. I didn't particularly care for such a bland fruit. It had to be laced with chilli and pepper to taste faintly of anything at all.

We did the Metro/Evening Standard crossword every day. We tried to complete it before we arrived home. We had become joint crossword masters because we both spotted different things. VF was great with Latin and complex words, I was better at clichés and other stuff.

The clue was 'pear-shaped fruit, seven letters'. I watched VF ponder and give up.

"Avocado, you twat."

"Avocado is not a pear shaped fruit."

"Yes it is, that is why they are called avocado pears."

"Bullshit, it's a teardrop shape."

They were definitely pear-shaped.

We spent another night in each other's arms. I left at 08:00 to head back to the Fens for a dental appointment. I finally got my teeth whitened as promised.

On the train home I ate hot porridge with almond butter and strawberry jam. The dentist poked my teeth with metal and I daydreamed of what to cook for VF next.

Baby ecstasy

A couple of days elapsed back in the Fens, alone. I spent the days listening to the radio and reading crime novels. I had binned my phone and all my worries. No bosses to call me up last minute, no stupid news articles, no need to photograph and document every meal. I grow in solitude. I loved it. My parents would be pissed off when they realised I didn't have a phone again. I often got rid of my phone then retrieved it in moments of desperation. I was on day three now, and loved it. Before you know it I'll be living off the grid skinning rabbits for dinner.

VF called the house last night to alert me of his movements. I didn't really care. It wasn't out of lack of love. It seemed insignificant to our relationship he had spent the day walking his friend's dog and making leek soup for dinner. I couldn't wait to end the call and get back to mailing my signed poetry books.

I got ready at a leisurely pace this morning and took my porridge with coffee whilst listening to the radio. Then I packaged up book orders ready for the post office. I was happy for reasons to go into town each day. My own little purpose. Today I was meeting my closest friend for coffee and a walk round Ely. We had just over a week's worth of gossip to catch up on and I sensed we both had a good deal to spill.

I wore my new cow print trainers as I wandered into town. I knew FG would love them. She loved clunky ugly '90s fashion.

I wondered how much the antidepressants would change me. Would I ditch cashmere flares for neon pink elastic leggings? I had gone from black leather brogues to cow print trainers— anything was possible. My doctor checked in with me this morning (not the one I was shagging three months ago). She warned me of a potential dip. She told me if the dip lasted more than a few days they might have to up my dose. I worried about the dip—the inevitable comedown. I had experienced it on drugs, alcohol, mania. I hated the thought of binning the cow print trainers and going back to brogues. I must be patient.

London had reentered Covid lockdown and I was not allowed to travel. I could sneakily use my nurse ID to catch a train, but that felt wrong. I missed the company of VF—the cuddles in bed, the freedom London brings—but everything seemed closed and glum. I would wait until Christmas to visit. Christmas is next week, I think.

The government had decided on a five day break in the rules to allow for festivities. VF, his brother and I would spend Christmas together in Notting Hill as a little family.

In another life I would have been angry I could not easily flee to London any more, but I no longer depended on VF for my happiness. I had the Fens, books and the radio.

I had not spent much time with family or friends in particular. Humans adapt fast. Covid was our new way of life. We all kept to ourselves, huddled up at home. Sometimes I felt I had been waiting my whole life for an excuse to stay indoors. Some people hated it, but the introverts cheered. The virus wouldn't do much harm to me or my friends, I didn't have older people in my life to worry about. My mother was the only vulnerable relative due to her poor lungs. I hope I didn't inherit her poor lungs. I love smoking. I smoked at every opportunity, switching between menthol and non-flavoured whenever one or the other started to bore me. I felt the same way about smoking as others feel about chocolate or sweets— I just craved it and cannot say no. I don't wish to encourage others or romanticise it, but I have few luxuries in life aside from smoking and reading.

Mulled wine

I crossed paths with two men I had dated in the past— only one or two dates. It turns out they had bonded over electronic music and formed a friendship after I knew them. We caught up over mulled wine in Cambridge beside the Mill Pond. One left, the other took me for a beer. We still weren't allowed indoors because of the virus, so again we drank outdoors on a bench until it was cold and dark.

I didn't remember too much about this one guy. I asked his age and it turned out he was 12 years older than I had guessed.

I did remember he gave me a foot massage on our first and only date. It was the best foot massage I have ever had. He cracked every knot right out. I love my feet being touched.

He had plans for the evening, else I would totally have gone back to his. I wasn't quite sure if I fancied him, but I would certainly let him touch my feet.

We went our separate ways and I drunkenly boarded a train home to the Fens. I was more drunk than I realised. I accidentally bumped into a woman whilst boarding.

I discovered several missed calls. I was happily tipsy and didn't fancy calling anyone back. I arrived home and went to bed at 19:00.

<u>Winter</u>

It felt like a typically cold dark winter day. I mostly stayed indoors watching TV and cooking. I began with a milky cup of coffee, then porridge with rhubarb jam, almond butter and blueberries. I fancied bananas but had none. The house felt cold so I warmed up with a milky rose black tea. I felt unusually hungry so I made six balls of stuffing with sage onion and pork, one roast parsnip and a dollop of cranberry sauce. It was delicious and comforting. I ate chocolate in the afternoon and glugged an Irn Bru.

At 15:00 I put on my makeup and strolled down to town, a 20 minute walk. I had checked the weather before I left, 10% chance of rain. It was dark by the time I left the house. I didn't mind.

I settled down in a coffee shop for the final hour before it closed. I drank steamed milk with chai spices. I didn't enjoy coffee this late.

Afterwards I would walk to meet an old friend at his house for tea. I hoped he had cake or crumpets—just something to nibble on. I am hungry today.

I can't remember why we fell out. He talked a lot but I knew nothing about him. I don't think we fell out, just drifted. I recall we tried to have sex once but it didn't work out. I barely recall.

He taught music at Cambridge and composed operas and stuff. I know very little about classical music. I was sure it would be nice to catch up, but I wasn't too excited. I am still not sure why he invited me over. I'd rather do a coffee shop. I couldn't remember much about his house except for a yellow wall, lots of books and a piano in the centre of the room topped with a stuffed white tiger.

Gin hangover

The composer and I drank gin, water and angostura bitters from dinky little glasses. We spoke about the modern obsession with phones, the Fens and past lovers. The white tiger still sat on the piano.

I walked home tipsy. I didn't enjoy the gin but had fancied a drink.

I slept fitfully for the second night in a row. I was scared I was dying. I would awake with terrible chest pains and nausea. It lasted half an hour before I drifted back off.

I watched TV in bed until 11:00. I absorbed a documentary about the Yorkshire Ripper. One episode seemed an entire feminist take. I do not like clubs. I refuse to be catalogued with half the population. I enjoy being a woman for the physical attributes, but I rarely think about gender. Perhaps that is what they call privilege nowadays—I don't have to think about it.

I contemplated walking into town for breakfast and a look around the market. It was six days until Christmas and I wanted to find a present for my mother before heading to London with VF. I wished I had someone to walk around the market with today.

I schlepped into town for lack of anything else to do. It was busy and the market only sold tat. I walked away annoyed and headed straight home. I hoped it wasn't the depression creeping back.

I packed four outfits and seven sets of underwear. I had bought no Christmas presents, I disliked gifts but bought them for my parents out of guilt. I certainly did not want anything for myself.

I planned to catch the train to London in the early evening.

Boris Johnson attempted to cancel Christmas by announcing the country was back under lockdown. I was happy to have already packed my bag. I threw on my boots and jumped onto the next train. I would see the Fens in the new year.

Dishes in the sink

I was annoyed not to start my day before 10:00. VF slept in and I spent two hours trying to crawl out of bed.

I made porridge for myself whilst VF ate an avocado, tomatoes and two poached eggs. One avocado down. I don't know why he bought so many. Like I said before, I hate them.

He spent close to two hours browsing the internet on his phone. If I even know what brand of phone you have you use it too much. I pictured how clean the house would be if he could avoid the internet for a day. But people have different priorities to me.

I poured myself a vodka and juice at 11:00. I needed a boost before our midday walk. VF wanted Hampstead Heath but I preferred Hyde Park. I drank my juice and thought about the dishes in the sink.

The vodka made the dishes a little easier to clean, but vodka didn't achieve what it used to. I danced around the house but just felt tired after my second drink. We walked to Portobello Road for star anise, cloves and cinnamon sticks for our mulled wine and cider. I was too tipsy to focus on anything but the need to pee.

Once home I slept for most of the afternoon. VF and I were getting on fine, but he often annoyed me. He would spend all day reading and I would scold him for it. He said I was cursing him for seeking more knowledge. I argued he let his life suffer because of this reading obsession. I pride myself on cleanliness to the point of obsession. But the pills help me feel more relaxed about clutter. Before I came to London I cleaned my house and washed all my bed linen for fear of how dreadful it might feel to return home to old, used bedsheets. Cleanliness is next to godliness. I always feel more calm and collected when just out of the bath.

I spent most of the afternoon reading as there was little else to do during the pandemic. All travel was now banned and I found myself stuck in London for two weeks or so. I wasn't sure I had made the right decision coming here. I loved VF dearly but it didn't feel passionate or romantic, It felt like the same old rhythm as the last two years. I wished I felt different. No other men had grabbed my attention. I had nothing to fight for, nor was I bothered.

I baked sweet potatoes for dinner with avocado and tomatoes. We drank a small glass of Montepulciano. I did the dishes whilst VF continued to read on the sofa. I was growing a little bored so I took a long, hot bath alone. It would have been pleasant if I hadn't heard the landlady upstairs. Every single fucking movement, the flush of her toilet, the taps running. I had noticed she didn't wash her hands for long. Following the sound of the flush, the tap would be on for just three seconds. It scares me to think people out there might listening in on my movements to see how long I wash my hands for. Maybe it was the nurse in me.

I don't have scales back at my house. VF's scales told me I weighed 11 pounds more than last year, my heaviest ever. I was delighted with this. Since quitting nursing I didn't have to run around everywhere. Instead I ate four small meals a day, read books and wrote.

I craved fruit. I bit into half a rancid lemon. I shared an orange with VF then made porridge with raspberry jam.

I had no plans for tomorrow. I should probably think about a job, but not quite sure what. I feel well enough to work nowadays—the PTSD has subsided. I sleep a normal amount and my moods are relatively stable.

Another month to myself would be perfect, as I still have money. I would love to find something small, local and part-time so I could afford a small flat with space for Nana Y's dining room table and two chairs I inherited. Until tomorrow.

The week of Christmas

I didn't want to write but had little else to do. My face was red and puffy for no reason but I would wear a mask and go to the supermarket anyway. Cooking was my only solace, whilst queues and supermarket food shortages abounded. England had become a stranded island. The factory that makes nothing.

It was raining and I didn't want to spend time with VF. I ate my porridge in silence and watched TV until mid-afternoon. He accused me of being snippy. VF needed a new focus. I thought a girlfriend might bring it. I worry not even a child would ground him.

I didn't want to go to the supermarket with him for fear VF would buy lots of shit we didn't need, like the current avocado fiasco. Who did that? It wasn't even funny.

He was right. I was in a shitty mood.

The trains are always late

I thought I was alright. My mood crashed every now and then which made me wonder if it was the company, the environment or just me at fault. I craved home, sitting in my small bedroom curling my hair, listening to the radio, reading my books. I am too much a woman of comfort. I stayed eight days and took the train home this morning.

It was a perfectly tolerable Christmas. I was drunk on two glasses of Cava and somehow made a delicious meal of sage stuffed pork loin and all the trimmings. I didn't want to eat meat anymore so vowed this would be the last time for a while. I smoked whilst I cooked and the boys watched a James Bond film. It was lovely, quiet and quaint.

The day before we had walked down to Hyde Park, me in my new wellies. They were navy blue with white polka dots. On the way we bought mulled wine on Portobello Road. The man at the stall light-heartedly mocked VF:

"I like this saying: thank you very much INDEED!"

He always said 'thank you very much indeed'.

I fed the squirrels, pigeons and parakeets by hand. A parakeet spent some time on my head. It made me broody for a child. I wanted someone to teach how to feed the birds. I should wait until I am at least 26.

We spent our days doing very little. Wary of my mood swings VF encouraged me to spend the days in bed reading before I emerged late afternoon for my bath and dinner. Last night I made roasted cumin cauliflower with chimichurri. This dish prompted a daydream. The daydream fuelled me for days and I kept returning to it. My own two-bedroom terraced house where I would cook for house guests or future boyfriends.

I planned the tablecloths I would buy, the plates I would use, and where I would source my row of perfectly matching spice jars (I decided M&S).

Perhaps the daydreams fuelled the depression. I had no job and no desire for one. I could no doubt claim money and even something for the PTSD, but that required more effort than I could summon energy for.

I needed a simple job in a shop—three days a week selling inoffensive kitchenware or perfume. But so far nothing. Dad advised me not to apply to the local parsnip factory as I'd be the sole woman there. That didn't bother me. I just wanted a job where I could get on without hassle and listen to the radio.

I was excited about my time back in the Fenlands. The sun had emerged for me. I worshipped the sun from the train window, despite knowing I'd be spending most of the future in my bedroom.

Most of the country (London and Fenlands included) was now back in lockdown after a scant few weeks of freedom. Covid numbers remained high despite the vaccination rollout. The shops were shut and we could meet just one person in an outside setting. I was glad. I had no plans to meet anyone. I am exhausted.

I had been speaking to God a lot and was relieved to bid goodbye to 2020. I spent the locked down days at home. I slept healthy amounts, watched TV, read and browsed the internet.

The planets seemed to have aligned. I bought a car, applied for a job and found an isolated village apartment in the Fens. It had two bedrooms and wooden floors throughout. Tomorrow I am picking up a vintage oak wardrobe that someone kindly donated. Life appeared to be back on track.

Two friends were working as community nurses. The pay was good. I too had applied.

Last night I slept 13 hours for no particular reason. I dreamt vividly of a girl my age with brown curly hair who I held in my arms. We sat in the corner of a pub talking. She was showing me the books she had written and illustrated. She was far more accomplished than me and I loved her work. We walked home arm in arm in the rain.

I awoke with a burning desire to find a girl to share my apartment and call my girlfriend. I felt these fleeting desires occasionally, I'd just never met the right woman.

VF had sent me an email last night before the year turned.

Dear Minnie Moo,

I just wanted to take this chance to properly wish you a Happy New Year.

It's been a crazy 12 months for so many people, I guess we are no exception.

I need you to know that I am incredibly proud of you.

There have been rough times but your indomitable spirit has seen you through.

I've no idea what 2021 holds for us but if we both stay diligent and focused I'm sure our lives will prosper and improve, and I'm sure some logic will emerge.

Love you dearly and with all my heart.

I found the letter to be very sweet, unthreatening and straightforward. I usually opened his emails with dread. Alcohol induced ramblings.

The email provoked no specific emotion. VF was my accomplice and almost a father figure. He took care of me, most of the time at least.

I often wondered how he would fit in if I were to find a serious boyfriend or girlfriend. I knew from experience finding someone was unlikely. I don't think I have ever met anyone truly interested in me. I am very young, I have time.

The dream made me want to put on a face of makeup, walk into town and hunt for a girlfriend. I knew it wouldn't work like that, especially in a Fenland town.

I would download a dating app on my iPad later on. I spent the rest of the day sleeping out of lockdown boredom (not depression).

Olives on the table

I left the house for my first real interaction during the lockdown. Covid numbers were escalating, with the NHS at breaking point. 58,000 cases yesterday, I read. I've not had it yet.

I spent most of the day watching TV and did a little exercise —a new hobby. 5kg weights, cycling then ab workout. I looked forward to my little exercise routine in the evening. It gave me something else to do whilst at home.

Today I feel a little hungover so the ab workout might be tough. I feel nauseous and am curled up on the sofa listening to Chopin.

So, last night. The classical pianist invited me over again. I want to call him 'piano man' but there is already a 'piano man' so I guess 'Ely piano man'. I arrived at 19:00. There were olives and crisps, then a green bean casserole. Dinner was particularly tasty. It was touching to see someone make such an effort for my little existence. Olives ready on the table. Real napkins (not paper)! A choice of drinks. Someone had prepared a meal in anticipation of my arrival, shopped for ingredients, hoovered the house. It was a touching gesture. This is what I craved from my romantic life. I had no particular romantic feelings for him, as we had simply been friends for four years.

The pigeon is asleep on the shelf.

I am too tired and hungover to write. This is another reason to question my memory of the night. We kissed once but it meant nothing.

I must sleep. I am not depressed though.

Job interview

I had spent a week in bed and had no plans to leave. I had crashed yet again. My doctor signed me off work so I could claim benefits without having to seek work. I'd been gifted a month in bed. I could not imagine a job interview.

I had a job interview for the community nursing job next week. I needed confidence for this job. This I do not have.

I went back to bed and closed the blinds.

Sorry, I am too ill to write.

<u>Do you care to know the date?</u>

I am conscious my diaries sound like those of a teenager. Often I worry I am stuck in this mindset. A teenage girl and not a woman. At least I now know where VF and I stand, have less reckless sex and more money.

I painted for the remainder of the day and wondered if writing really was for me. Right now it served as an idiotic diary of my mistakes and dumb men.

I craved a date with a friend. Baked pastry and a walk. Hot coffee on cold benches. I strolled in Regent's Park with a man I no longer talk to.

Afterwards I went to see the Glaswegian. We did a lot of coke, listened to music and I never made it to the job interview.

Up north

I am certainly better.

I spent a few days in Liverpool. Wherever I go, I feel homeless. I have worn the same outfit for three weeks, rotating four pairs of pants.

In Liverpool my childhood friend PB and I ate fried chicken and did a lot of coke, which rendered me almost motionless for several days. I did manage to stroll past the twin cathedrals and sit by the docks. The birds were too loud and I couldn't find anywhere open that sold coffee. I drank juice and watched the dogs in the cathedral grounds.

My train arrived into Euston late. VF was waiting on the wrong platform. The mistake bothered me. It made me think London didn't want me. Liverpool didn't want me either.

I felt I should head back to Fenland tomorrow to sort out my affairs, get laid and find some peace.

Peace.

Neither London nor Liverpool offered it.

I vow to go home tomorrow.

Finishing things

I spent one night with VF. I cooked lemon garlic prawns with lots of chilli on bread. We drank dry white wine and talked all evening.

In the morning I walked across town to Lancaster Gate to finish compiling the diaries. The studio is very cold but it is opposite Hyde Park, where I can eat lunch.

I am none the wiser about myself or the diaries. VF is picking me up for lunch at 15:00 in the Italian gardens by the fountain.

We nearly made love this morning, but not quite.

I think it must be over for good.

Acknowledgements

There are people who have influenced this book far more than any of my lovers.

They include Martha Gellhorn and her *Travels with Myself and Another* alongside Anaïs Nin and *The Diary of Anaïs Nin*.

The act of writing is not a solo mission. I give thanks to my editors Ronnie Angel Pope and Jonathan Gilbert.

Thank you for making my words and thoughts brighter.

This book contains themes of mental illness and references to suicide. If you are affected by any of the themes discussed I encourage you to contact Samaritans.

When life is difficult, Samaritans are here—day or night, 365 days a year. You can call them for free on 116 123, email them at jo@samaritans.org, or visit www.samaritans.org to find your nearest branch.

Other international helplines can be found at www.befrienders.org.

Printed in Great Britain
by Amazon